WHY DO OUR BODIES STOP GROWING?

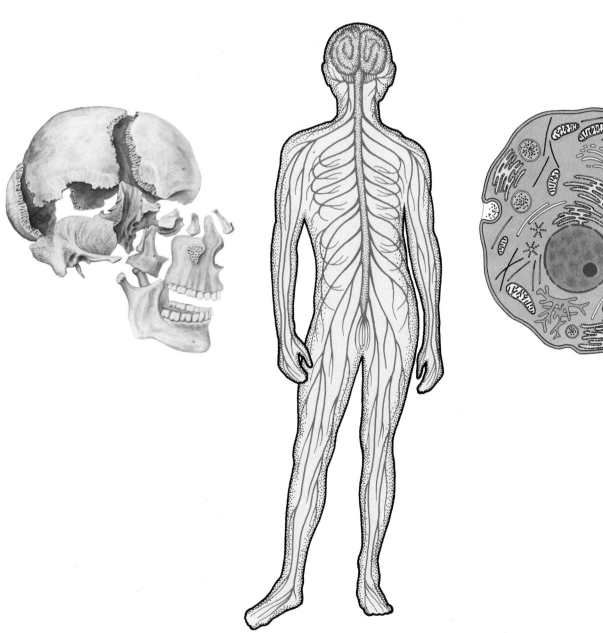
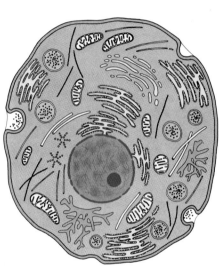

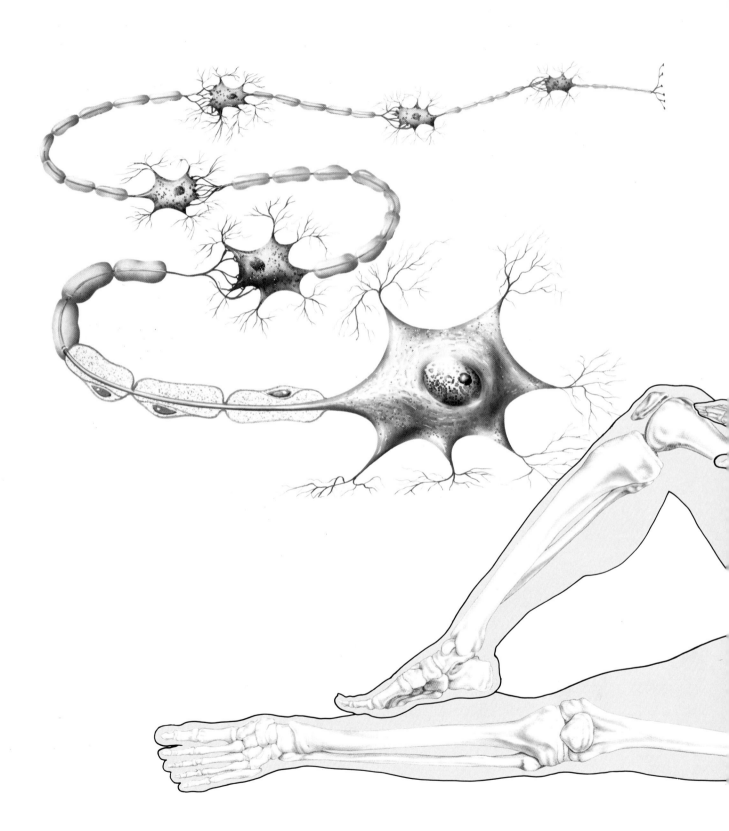

WHY DO OUR BODIES STOP GROWING?

Questions about human anatomy
answered by the
Natural History Museum

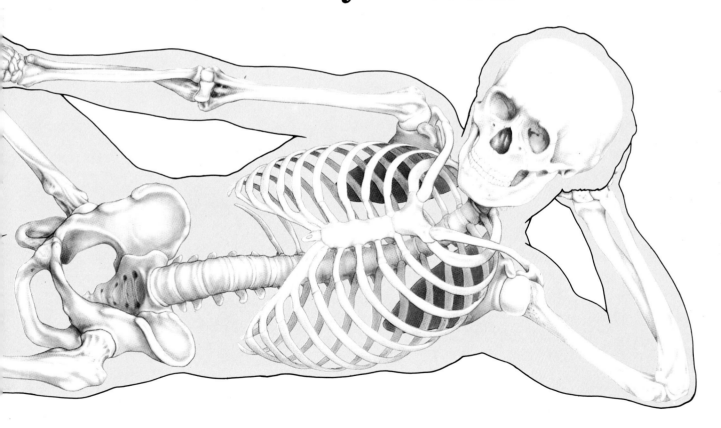

Dr Philip Whitfield & Dr Ruth Whitfield

Viking Kestrel

VIKING KESTREL
Published by the Penguin Group
Viking Penguin Inc., 40 West 23rd Street, New York, New York 10010, U.S.A.
Penguin Books Ltd, 27 Wrights Lane, London W8 5TZ, England
Penguin Books Australia Ltd, Ringwood, Victoria, Australia
Penguin Books Canada Ltd, 2801 John Street, Markham, Ontario, Canada L3R 1B4
Penguin Books (N.Z.) Ltd, 182–190 Wairau Road, Auckland 10, New Zealand

Penguin Books Ltd, Registered Offices: Harmondsworth, Middlesex, England

First published in 1988 by Viking Penguin Inc.
Published simultaneously in Canada

Why Do Our Bodies Stop Growing?
was conceived, edited and designed by
Marshall Editions Limited
170 Piccadilly
London W1V 9DD

Copyright © Marshall Editions Limited, 1988
All rights reserved

Editor
Carole McGlynn

Art Editor
Eddie Poulton

Picture Editor
Zilda Tandy

Managing Editor
Ruth Binney

Production
Barry Baker
Janice Storr

Library of Congress catalog card number: 88-80669
(CIP data available)
ISBN 0-670-82331-7

Printed and bound in Spain
by Cayfosa Industria Gráfica
Barcelona

1 2 3 4 5 92 91 90 89 88

Contents

Introduction

Why Do Our Bodies Stop Growing? answers the vital questions about the anatomy of your body and the way it works. With the help of its fascinating illustrations, it looks inside the body and, system by system, explains why we are built in the way we are.

The book describes the building blocks of the body at every level – the organs, tissues, cells, and even the specialized chemical molecules that make up your millions of microscopic cells. It also explains the ways in which all these parts of the human machine actually work – the fuels it needs, its wastes, its controls, its defenses, and its repair systems.

Often, we take our own bodies for granted. Most of the time they seem to work perfectly well without us thinking about them. When your body needs food for energy or for making you grow, you feel hungry and you eat. When it needs rest, you feel drowsy – then you go to sleep. When it has lost a lot of fluid, you find you are thirsty. If you need to pick something up, you can do it instantly. Without a moment's concentration, your eyes have pinpointed the object's position and your arms and fingers have moved to get it. Your body can do all these things – and thousands of others – without you having to worry how it does them.

Watch the clumsy movements of an industrial robot, controlled by a large computer, as it tries to pick up a small object that it has not been programmed to deal with. Then compare its hopeless fumbling with what you can do without trying. You will then realize, if you did not before, that the human body is an almost miraculous piece of bioengineering.

So, if you have ever wondered what your liver is for, why blood is red, how broken bones manage to mend, where tears come from, or how your body knows when to stop growing, this book will give you the answers.

1

Is skin alive?

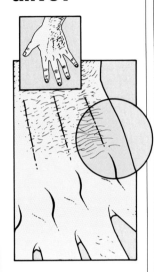

The outside of your skin is, in fact, dead, but just underneath the surface it is very much alive.

Your skin is made in layers and it grows as you grow. Only a fraction of an inch (less than a millimeter) below the surface, at the bottom of the layer called the epidermis, skin cells are continually splitting and producing new ones. These are gradually pushed up to the surface of the skin, a journey which usually takes three to four weeks.

As the cells progress upward, they get filled with a tough protein called keratin, which makes skin waterproof and germproof. These skin cells slowly flatten and harden as they move up, and they eventually die as they reach the outer surface.

This means that the surface of the skin is made up of dead keratin cells called skin scales. When these fall off the scalp we call them dandruff, but they are also constantly being shed from other parts of your body as well. They rub off as you wash yourself, dry yourself with a towel and move around. A large proportion of "house dust" is made up of dead skin scales.

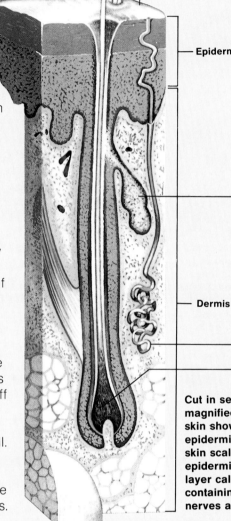

- Hair
- Skin surface
- Epidermis
- Sebaceous gland
- Dermis
- Sweat gland
- Hair root (follicle)

Cut in section and highly magnified, this piece of skin shows the living epidermis, topped by dead skin scales. Below the epidermis is a thicker layer called the dermis, containing blood vessels, nerves and sweat glands.

2

Why is black skin black and white skin white?

The color of a person's skin is due to the color-producing cells at the base of the epidermis. These cells, called melanocytes, produce the colored substance melanin, which is dark brown to black.

Apart from albinos (totally white-skinned people), who have none of these cells, everyone has melanocytes. The differences in skin color are due to the widely varying amounts of melanin these cells produce. If they produce little, the skin is "white" (really a light pink or buff shade). At the other extreme, if they produce a lot, the skin looks dark brown or black. There are of course hundreds of shades in between.

Melanin protects the skin from the effects of too much sun by shading its deeper layers. People from hot, sunny places tend to have darker skin, like the people of tropical Africa. Their black skin is good protection against the dangerous ultraviolet rays in strong sunlight.

People from cooler climates are fairer-skinned since they do not need this protection. Freckles, which tend to occur in light-skinned people, happen when the melanin gathers in clusters.

Why does skin get tanned in the sun?

Nestling among the dividing cells at the base of the epidermis is a color-producing melanocyte. In this magnified view it looks like a spotted octopus. Its "tentacles" pass colored granules to the more rounded ordinary skin cells. In this way black coloration is spread upward through the skin in tanning.

Tanning is a protective trick used by the skin. It helps the surface of the body avoid the dangerous effects of too much sun by absorbing the sun's harmful ultraviolet rays.

People of every skin color darken when they are exposed to large amounts of sunlight: even the skin of black people turns a deeper shade. What happens is that the melanocytes at the bottom of the epidermis produce more melanin in the form of tiny black granules.

Some of these granules stay inside the producer cells. Others are spread through the surrounding cells of the epidermis. All newly-darkened cells then begin their journey to the surface of the skin, which takes only four to five days. The thicker coating of dark color protects the skin and produces the tan.

Dead flattened
keratin cells
of epidermis

Melanin granules

Living epidermal
cell

Melanin-containing
cell (melanocyte)

Why do my fingers go wrinkled in the bath?

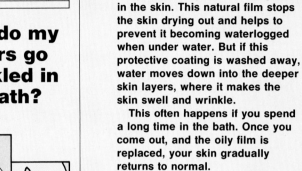

Skin is covered with a thin film of oil, produced by sebaceous glands in the skin. This natural film stops the skin drying out and helps to prevent it becoming waterlogged when under water. But if this protective coating is washed away, water moves down into the deeper skin layers, where it makes the skin swell and wrinkle.

This often happens if you spend a long time in the bath. Once you come out, and the oily film is replaced, your skin gradually returns to normal.

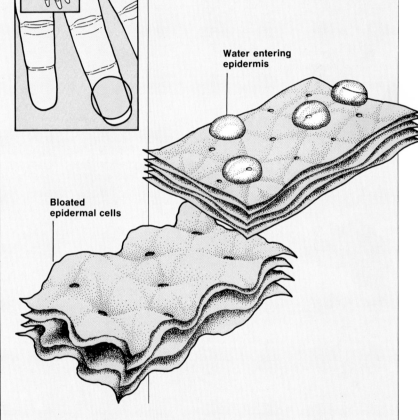

Water entering
epidermis

Bloated
epidermal cells

Because you stay in the water too long! Normally, the dead outer layers of skin are strong and waterproof, protecting the tissues underneath. Their strength comes from the tough, flexible protein called keratin of which they are made. Their waterproofing is due to a film of oil, known as sebum, on the skin surface.

But warm, soapy bath water removes this oily film and eventually lets water seep into the dead skin cells underneath. Swollen with water, this layer puckers up into the pale wrinkles that you get when you lie in the bath for too long.

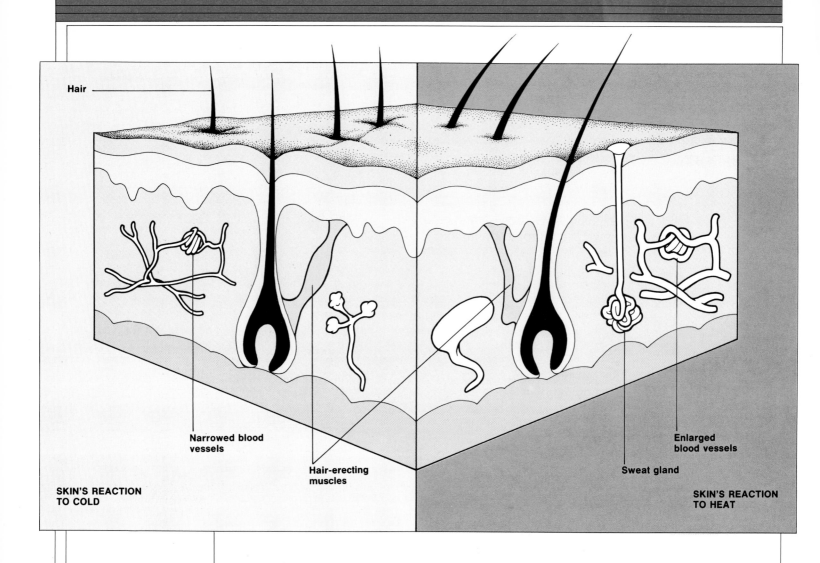

Hair

Narrowed blood
vessels

Hair-erecting
muscles

Enlarged
blood vessels

Sweat gland

**SKIN'S REACTION
TO COLD**

**SKIN'S REACTION
TO HEAT**

5

Why do I get "goose bumps" when I'm cold?

The goose bumps—or goose pimples—are trying to keep you warm!

All mammals—warm-blooded, hairy animals that feed their young with milk—are covered in hair. All, that is, with a few exceptions like ourselves, whales and dolphins. We wear clothes and live inside heated homes to keep warm, while whales and dolphins use the thick layer of fat in their skin to conserve their body heat.

When any furry mammal gets cold, its hair automatically "stands on end," which makes its fur coat thicker and more warming by trapping inside it a deeper layer of air. This insulating air works like a blanket, and keeps the creature warm.

Your own skin is more or less bare, but most of your body is covered in fine, very short hairs. Even though we are mammals,

we are not furry, but when we are cold our few hairs stand on end, too. When they stick up, a little bump of skin—a goose bump—springs up at the base of each hair. The bump is formed because the muscle that pulls the hair upright bunches up the skin as well.

Because our hairy coat is so feeble, the goose-bump changes do not really help to keep us warm. But we cannot stop these changes happening: they are what is called a reflex. They occur quite automatically, as though that part of your body was under "autopilot" control.

Getting cold will also make you shiver—another reflex that happens whether you want it to or not. Shivering is of some use, however, because it produces heat in your muscles.

6

What causes pimples?

Pimples are inflammations of the skin caused by tiny infections from germs. The easiest place for germs to invade the body is through the holes where the hairs on your skin poke out.

Pimples occur particularly when the hair base or follicle is blocked up by extra amounts of the waxy skin substance, sebum. Bacteria in the adjacent sebaceous glands break down the trapped sebum into chemicals known as fatty acids. These acids irritate the hair follicle, then cause it to burst. The sebum and acids inflame the skin and a pimple appears on the skin surface, as a spot or blackhead.

Acne, or a rash of pimples over the face, neck and back, is especially common in the early teenage years of adolescence.

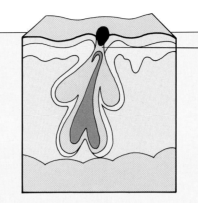

Blocked hair follicle

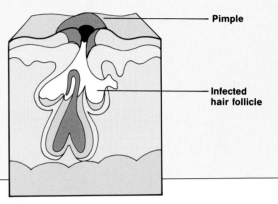

Pimple

Infected hair follicle

7

Why do I sweat when I'm hot?

Sweating is an automatic response by an overheated body, and it is trying to cool you down. You sweat if your body gets too hot, whether this is caused by being in a hot place or by strenuous exercise.

Sweat is a salty, watery liquid made in long curly sweat glands buried in the deeper layer of the skin, called the dermis. The sweat reaches the surface of the skin via minute skin pores connected by tubes to the sweat glands.

When you get hot, the blood-carrying tubes or vessels in the skin get bigger, and more liquid passes from them into the sweat glands. The glands make more sweat and it flows up to the skin surface. At the surface, the sweat evaporates, and in doing so it draws heat from your body to cool it down.

Dogs have no sweat glands. In hot weather they pant, with their tongues out, in order to cool themselves down.

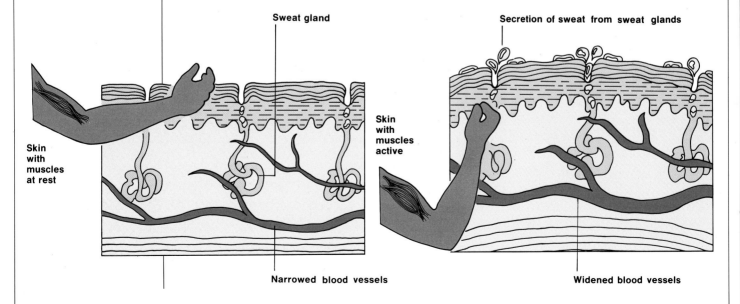

Sweat gland

Secretion of sweat from sweat glands

Skin with muscles at rest

Skin with muscles active

Narrowed blood vessels

Widened blood vessels

8

How do cuts heal themselves?

When you cut your skin, you take it for granted that the cut will gradually heal and the skin finally mend itself. But the way this happens is a complicated task carried out by both skin and blood working together.

Think what happens to a cut finger. The cut bleeds, then the blood in the cut clots, or sets, and dries to form a scab on the surface of the skin. Under the scab new skin starts forming, which you can see once the hardened, dried scab falls off.

The first important step in all these changes is the clotting of the blood. The clot stops more blood escaping from the wound and, by plugging the hole, it helps prevent dirt and germs from entering the body. The clot or plug is formed in the first instance by tiny pieces of cells called platelets. There are billions of these in the bloodstream and when they come to a cut they stick to each other and to the edges of the cut to make a thin seal over it.

At the same time platelets send out chemical messages that bring about the making of the main clot. These signals cause fibers of the clotting protein, called fibrin, to form. The fibers make a dense criss-crossing mesh in the cut and this network of fibers is the clot. Soon it starts to shrink, pulling the sides of the cut together. At the skin's surface the fibrin clot dries out in the air and makes a scab.

Both under and in the clot, new skin cells move across the gap caused by the cut. These cells multiply and soon make brand new skin which will be ready when the scab falls off, a few days later.

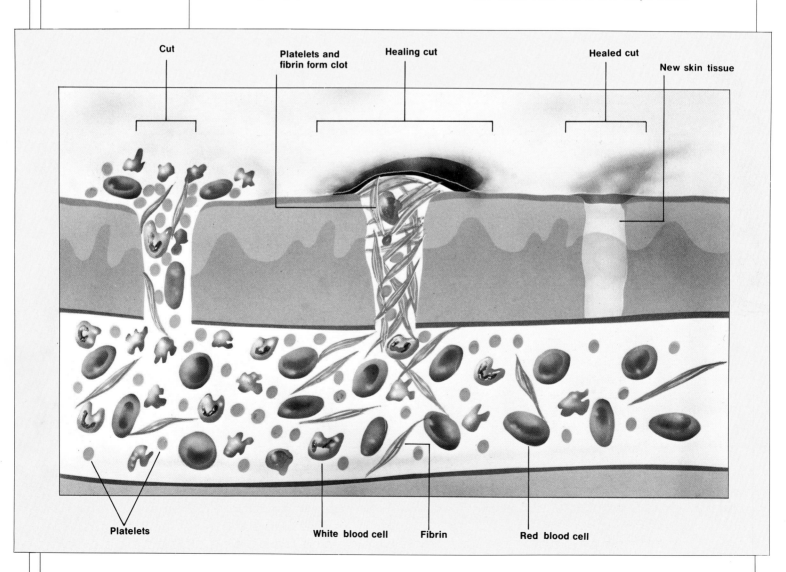

Cut

Platelets and fibrin form clot

Healing cut

Healed cut

New skin tissue

Platelets

White blood cell

Fibrin

Red blood cell

Why don't I have hair all over my body?

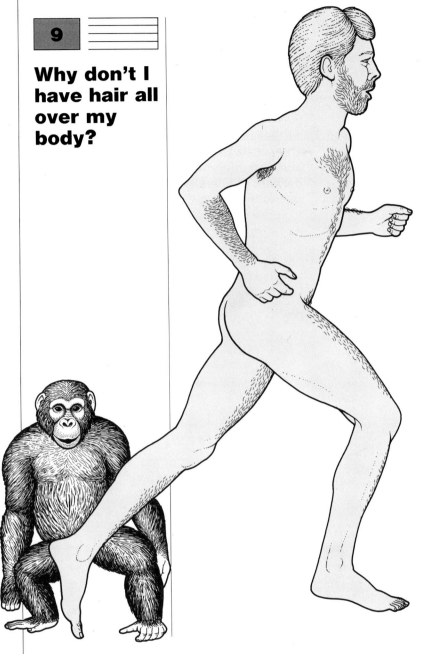

Why does hair come in different shades?

The color of your hair is decided by what you inherited from your parents—hair colors are passed on from generation to generation.

As with skin color, the color of hair is due to varying amounts of the colored substance called melanin in the hairs themselves. There is a dark brown melanin and a reddish melanin. Depending on the proportions of the two in your hair, the final color can be any shade between fair and black —or it may be ginger.

Blondes have hair with tiny amounts of melanin; redheads possess only the reddish color. Gray or white hair contains no melanin. In old age no melanin is added to new growing hairs. So they turn white if the hair was originally fair, or gray if it was dark.

Why do some people go bald?

Most people who have lost their hair are elderly.

In old age a number of changes happen to the skin. It gets more wrinkled as it loses its elasticity. It also becomes drier. The hairs in the skin are made without melanin pigment and so they are gray or white in color.

In the end, particularly in men, no new hairs are made to replace those that fall out and they slowly go bald.

A few younger people also become bald, especially if this runs in the family. Illness can also make the hair fall out at an early age.

Although our close relatives in the animal world such as the chimpanzee have hair all over their bodies, all we have left is a few patches. Children have hair only on their heads and eyebrows. Adults grow extra hair under the armpits, around the genitals and, if men, on their faces. Some men also develop more body hair, especially on the chest, legs and arms.

Our hair is not really any use for keeping us warm. But the hair we have kept is probably for signalling to each other. Eyebrows accentuate the eyes, beards and body hair distinguish men from women.

It is quite possible that in our early evolution, one or two million years ago, these hair patterns were more important to survival than they are now.

12

Why do we have two sets of teeth?

We have two sets of teeth so that our teeth are always the right size for our mouths. Once teeth have fully emerged from the gums they get no bigger. A tooth grows only while being made under the gums.

Your first set of teeth are called baby teeth or milk teeth. They started being formed, out of sight, during the middle months of your mother's pregnancy. By the time you were born, both upper and lower front (incisor) teeth were already formed but hidden under your gums. You "cut" these teeth when you were roughly a year old. By about two years of age your full set of 20 milk teeth was in place.

Between the ages of five and ten your milk teeth become loose and fall out, one at a time, starting with the front ones. They are replaced by more, larger adult teeth. These fit your jaws, which have now developed and are much bigger than they were when you were a baby. But the very back teeth, the back molars, will not erupt for another ten years.

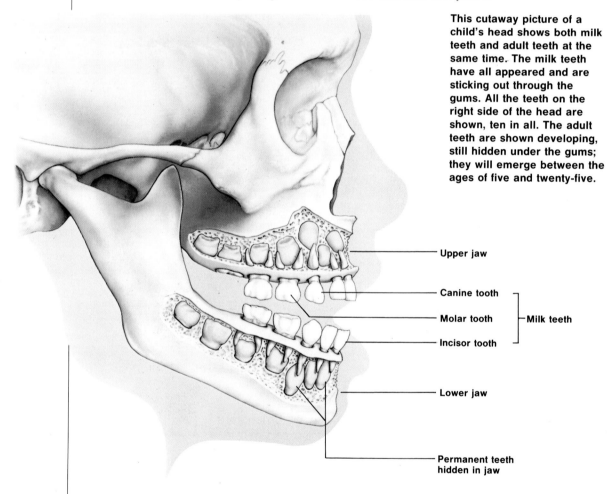

This cutaway picture of a child's head shows both milk teeth and adult teeth at the same time. The milk teeth have all appeared and are sticking out through the gums. All the teeth on the right side of the head are shown, ten in all. The adult teeth are shown developing, still hidden under the gums; they will emerge between the ages of five and twenty-five.

Upper jaw

Canine tooth

Molar tooth — Milk teeth

Incisor tooth

Lower jaw

Permanent teeth hidden in jaw

13

What are wisdom teeth and when will I get them?

The four wisdom teeth are the last adult teeth to come through. They usually appear between the ages of 15 and 25.

The 20 baby teeth in a child's mouth are eventually replaced by 32 adult teeth. The rearmost flat, grinding teeth at the back of each jaw (upper and lower) come last. It is because these four back molars come out around the time that most people stop growing that they are called "wisdom teeth"—the idea being that you are wise by this time.

In some people, the wisdom teeth stay tucked away under the gums for ever. You can manage reasonably well without the wisdom teeth, since you would still have lots of other teeth with which to chew and crush your food. Nor does it mean that you are any the less wise if your wisdom teeth never appear!

14
What are my teeth made of?

A tooth is made of many parts. The near-white part you see when you look at your mouth with a mirror, is the outer layer called enamel. This is the hardest substance in the body—tougher even than bone. It has to be because the surface enamel of an adult tooth has to last from the time the tooth appears for nearly the whole of your life.

The enamel covers only the "crown" of a tooth—the part that sticks out above the gum. Inside the enamel is another layer of hard material called dentine, which can absorb bumps and knocks. Inside the dentine is the sensitive part of each tooth called the pulp.

The pulp contains blood vessels that keep the inner part of the tooth alive. It also has nerves, which mean that you can feel pain in a tooth if it is banged or has decay. The pulp stretches through the middle of a tooth's roots so that the blood vessels and nerves can connect up with those of the jaw.

15
Why do teeth sometimes need filling?

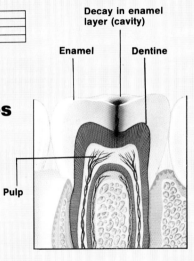

Decay in enamel layer (cavity)

Enamel **Dentine**

Cavity drilled and "filling" replaces decayed enamel

Pulp

A tooth needs filling when decay destroys a part of it. Decay starts when acid slowly eats away the protective layer of tooth enamel. A hole appears in the enamel and eventually spreads through to the dentine and pulp.

The acid is a waste product formed when germs (bacteria), which are always present in the mouth, break down sugars in the food debris left in the mouth after eating.

A dentist mends decay by drilling out any damaged dentine and enamel and plugging the cavity with a "filling" made of hard plastic or an amalgam of metals.

16
How can I look after my teeth so that I don't lose them?

Caring for your teeth and gums involves brushing them after meals, eating a sensible diet and visiting a dentist regularly to have your teeth checked. This will reduce the likelihood of fillings, and you will eventually lose few, if any, teeth.

Do not eat too many sweet or sticky foods or syrupy drinks. Always brush your teeth thoroughly after a meal and before you go to bed. This "washing" removes the sugars from which bacteria make the acids that cause tooth decay.

Cleaning the teeth with a toothbrush and dental floss, a length of waxed string, removes food particles and the substance called "plaque" from the surfaces of the teeth. It is equally important to clean between the teeth and the gums beneath.

The enamel of teeth can be toughened by fluoride, a mineral present in some drinking water. Where the water contains insufficient quantities, children can take a fluoride pill or drops each day.

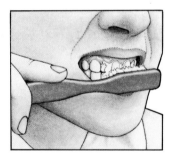

Cleaning with a toothbrush is the best way of removing plaque from the teeth. Your dentist will show you the most effective way of brushing.

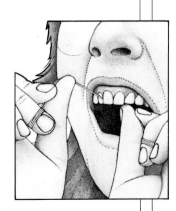

Running dental floss between the teeth pulls out food fragments which are difficult to reach with a brush. Floss also keeps the gums healthy.

How many bones are there in my body?

An adult's body contains 206 separate bones but, surprisingly, the younger you are, the more bones you have. A newborn baby has about 350 bones, but as he or she grows, many join together to make fewer, larger bones. A scientist can make a very close guess at the age of a child just by looking at an X-ray of the skeleton.

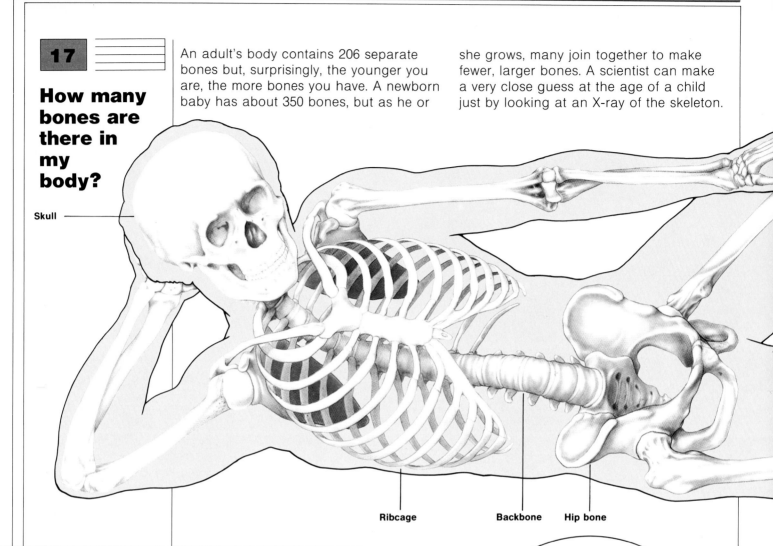

Skull

Ribcage   Backbone   Hip bone

How many bones are there in my hand?

The complicated movements that you can make with your hand are made possible by its 27 separate bones, all intricately linked together with muscles, tendons and ligaments.

Eight wrist bones (carpals) are joined together in a more or less solid block, while the bones of the palm and fingers are separate and more mobile. Four metacarpal bones make up the palm itself.

The metacarpal bone of the thumb can move sideways, which enables the thumb to turn around to touch each of the fingers. This allows us to grip small objects between finger and thumb in a "pincer grip."

The smaller bones of the fingers and thumb are called phalanges.

Finger bones (phalanges)

Thumb bone

Palm bones (metacarpals)

Wrist bones (carpals)

This is because the bones join together at a steady rate and in a strict order.

The bones of the skeleton come in a variety of shapes and sizes which suit them for their particular jobs. At one extreme are the thigh bones (the femurs), which are the body's biggest bones, and support its weight. At the other extreme are the tiny bones called ossicles in the middle ear, which carry sound vibrations from the eardrum deep into the ear. They are so small that a surgeon needs a microscope to operate on them accurately.

All these bones, whether small or large, are living structures made from a mixture of bone cells and a hard mineral "cement."

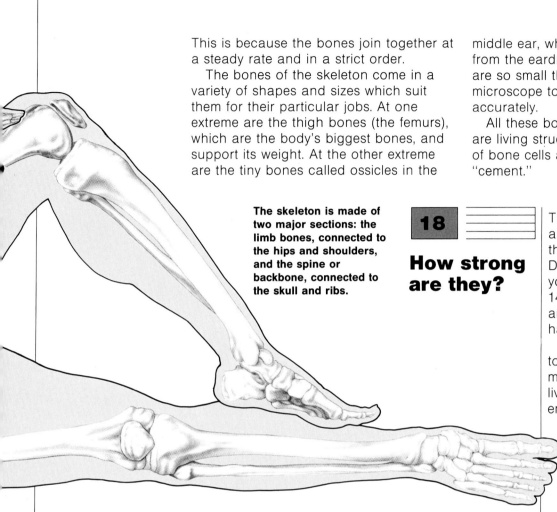

The skeleton is made of two major sections: the limb bones, connected to the hips and shoulders, and the spine or backbone, connected to the skull and ribs.

Toe bones (phalanges)

Arch bones (metatarsals)

Ankle bones (tarsals)

18
How strong are they?

The skeleton makes a strong and flexible framework for all the other organs of the body. Despite this heavyweight job, your bones make up only about 14 per cent of your weight – or around 20 lb (9 kg) once you have stopped growing.

Each bone is made of tough, fibrous proteins and a mineral "cement" in which living bone cells are embedded. This mixed structure makes bones strong but light. Steel bars of the same strength as bones would weigh five times as much.

20
Does my foot have the same number?

Almost the same number. Each foot has, in fact, one bone fewer than your hand, totalling 26. The difference in the number of bones occurs in the ankle region – the foot's equivalent of the wrist – where there are seven rather than eight bones.

The tarsal (ankle) and metatarsal bones form the arch of your foot. Its curved shape ensures that your body's weight is spread – some taken by the heel and some by your toes – as you walk or stand.

Toes are, of course, much shorter than fingers: that alone makes them far less flexible and mobile.

Very high-heeled shoes spoil this neat piece of bone design by throwing all of the body's weight on the toes. If worn for a long time, they can damage your toes.

What are bones made of?

Bones are made of mineral crystals, proteins and cells. These elements are woven together to make an incredibly strong yet light framework for the soft, flexible tissues of the body. Without bones, your body would slump on the floor like a rag doll or a "sagbag."

Every bone in the human body is made up of two types of bone. One type, compact bone, is solid and smooth like marble. The other type is lighter and spongy and is called cancellous bone.

In a long bone, like the thigh bone (the femur), the two types of bone are in specific places. The bone as a whole is a hollow tube with soft, jellylike marrow in its center. The marrow is a food store for fats and a place where new blood cells are made. The main wall of the bone tube is made of compact bone.

At each end of the bone there is a solid knob, or head; this is where the bones meet, at joints. The heads are made of spongy cancellous bone. Here the strands of bone in its spongy core are arranged in beautiful curving patterns that enable the femur to bear stresses that come from carrying the body's weight around.

Wrapped around all of the outside of the bone is a thin skinlike membrane. It is rich in blood vessels which nourish the bone inside and it forms an anchorage for the muscles and joints that attach to the bone. It also contains many nerves. Pain from a broken bone comes mainly from the nerves in a damaged membrane.

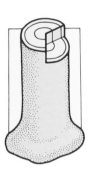

The solid part of bone is a mixture of mineral crystals and tough protein (collagen) fibers. These are arranged in bands like tree rings around thin channels called Haversian canals. Each minute rod of bone with a canal at its center is called a Haversian system.

The canals carry blood and foods to the tiny bone cells that lie among the "tree rings." Bundles of Haversian systems make up strong, solid bone.

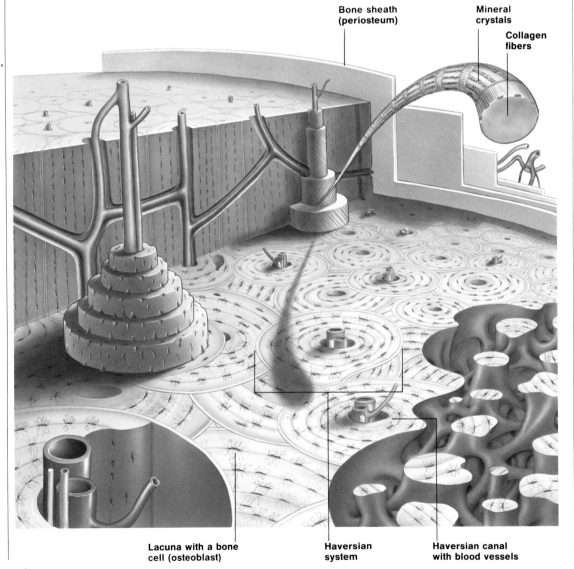

Bone sheath (periosteum)

Mineral crystals

Collagen fibers

Lacuna with a bone cell (osteoblast)

Haversian system

Haversian canal with blood vessels

How do joints work?

Wherever two next door bones have to move, a joint is needed and there are several different types of joint in the body. The joint between bones is usually surrounded by a bag of tissue called a joint capsule. This serves two purposes. It keeps the ends of the bones in place but it also holds a liquid called synovial fluid which lubricates the bone ends.

The fluid acts like oil in a car, enabling the bones to slide over each other smoothly. The ends of the bones in the joint are coated with a super-slippery or "non-stick" substance called cartilage.

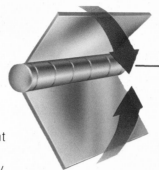

Like the hinge on a door, the elbow joint between the forearm and the upper arm allows movement in only one direction.

The joint at the base of the thumb enables it to be very mobile. This type of joint is called a saddle joint.

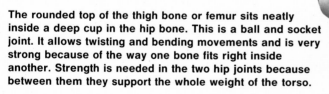

The rounded top of the thigh bone or femur sits neatly inside a deep cup in the hip bone. This is a ball and socket joint. It allows twisting and bending movements and is very strong because of the way one bone fits right inside another. Strength is needed in the two hip joints because between them they support the whole weight of the torso.

Linking the bones in the foot between the toes and the ankle are flattened sliding joints. They do not permit very much movement, but they do give this part of the foot the flexibility it needs to adjust itself to the strains and stresses of running or supporting your body's weight.

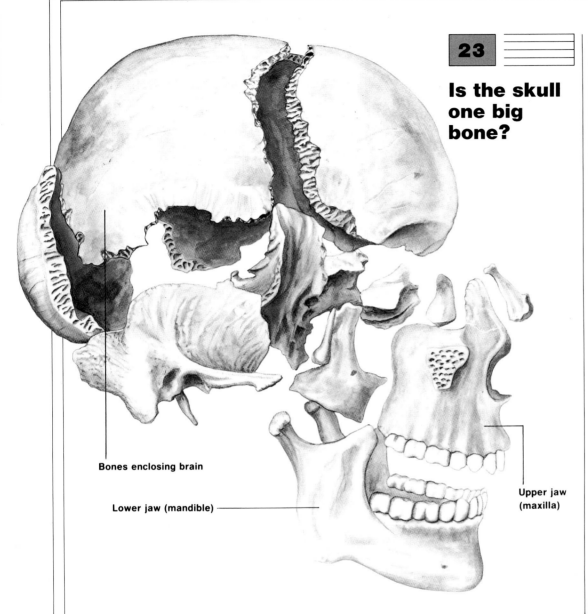

Bones enclosing brain

Lower jaw (mandible)

Upper jaw (maxilla)

Is the skull one big bone?

The skull is the name for all the bones in the head. Although when you see a skull on a skeleton, it looks as though it is a single bone, it is in fact made up of 22 smaller bones. But they fit together so tightly that they appear to be one.

Most of the skull bones are joined together, or "fused," for strength, as the skull's main job is to protect the soft brain inside it. The joints, called sutures, between the bones are made up of wavy edges that interlock like pieces in a jigsaw puzzle.

Attached to the skull is the only bone you can feel with ease, the lower jaw or mandible. It pivots on hinge joints just in front of your ears when you open your mouth to breathe, talk or eat.

Although most of the skull looks as if it is one large bone, it is in fact made of several bones joined together. This picture, however, has been drawn to show the individual bones as if they were spread apart.

Why do we walk on two legs when other animals walk on four?

Walking on two legs has a number of clear advantages. It gets your head, nose, ears and eyes as high above the ground as possible. This arrangement is ideal for giving all your sense organs, especially your eyes, the maximum range to work in. Up on two legs you can see distant food or danger more easily. Two-legged animals can usually run and change direction very quickly.

For human beings, walking on our hind legs has freed our fore-legs – or arms as we call them – for other things. With sensitive, mobile fingers on the ends of each hand, we can use our fore-limbs for holding and moving things with great precision.

If our arms had to be efficient for walking and running on the ground as well, they would probably perform the other jobs far less successfully. Hooves are not much use for writing, drawing or peeling bananas!

Human beings are not the only good two-legged walkers. Ostriches and kangaroos and, for some of the time, gorillas and chimpanzees, also move in this way. Extinct dinosaurs such as *Tyrannosaurus* used the same means of getting about.

How do broken bones mend?

Bones are living structures and have an amazing ability to repair themselves when they break or fracture. The healing takes place naturally, but it happens most swiftly and safely if the broken bone is held in one position. That is why plaster and splints are used.

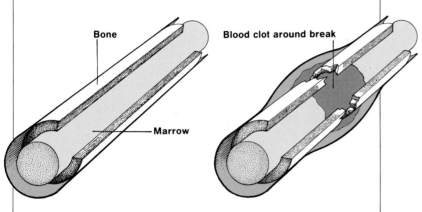

Bone

Marrow

Blood clot around break

When a bone breaks, the first part of the healing process is the formation of a large blood clot all around the break. The blood for the clot comes from the cut blood vessels in the bone marrow.

Secondly, a cuff of cartilage called a callus forms around the break. This holds the two halves of bone firmly together like a natural splint. New bone then grows out into the callus from both sides until a new section is made in the break.

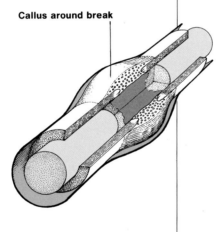

Callus around break

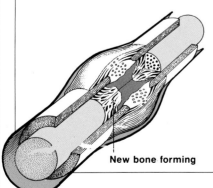

New bone forming

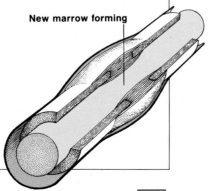

New marrow forming

26 Do bones ever wear out?

Bones hardly ever wear out, but the joints between them can show signs of wear and tear in old age, and this can produce damage at the bone ends. In older people with arthritis, the damaged joints are painful and swollen and cannot be moved properly.

The hip joint between the hip and upper leg bone (the femur), is often affected in this way. Luckily it is also one of the joints that can easily be replaced by surgery. A new stainless steel "head" is fitted to the end of the femur. It moves smoothly in a cup of slippery plastic joined to the hip bone.

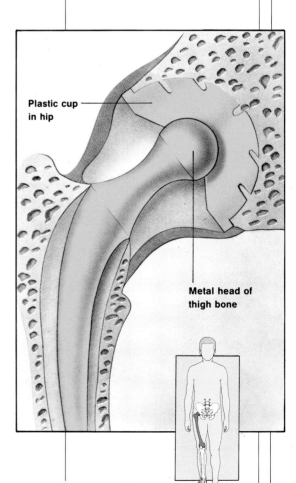

Plastic cup in hip

Metal head of thigh bone

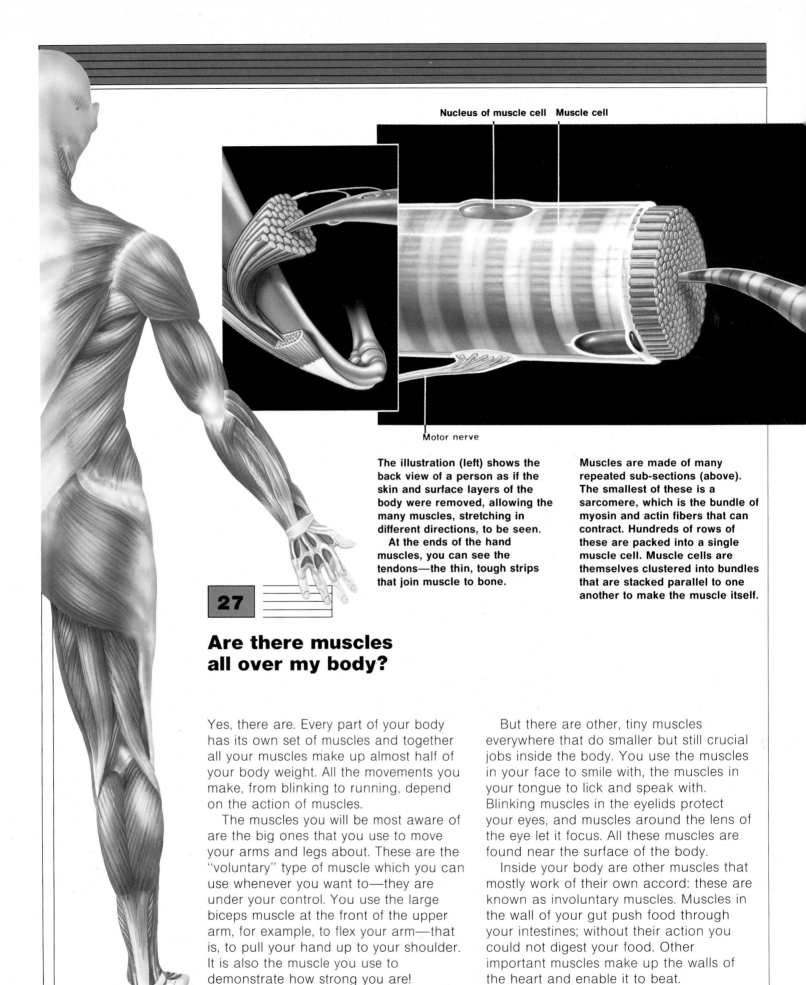

Nucleus of muscle cell   Muscle cell

Motor nerve

The illustration (left) shows the back view of a person as if the skin and surface layers of the body were removed, allowing the many muscles, stretching in different directions, to be seen.

At the ends of the hand muscles, you can see the tendons—the thin, tough strips that join muscle to bone.

Muscles are made of many repeated sub-sections (above). The smallest of these is a sarcomere, which is the bundle of myosin and actin fibers that can contract. Hundreds of rows of these are packed into a single muscle cell. Muscle cells are themselves clustered into bundles that are stacked parallel to one another to make the muscle itself.

27

Are there muscles all over my body?

Yes, there are. Every part of your body has its own set of muscles and together all your muscles make up almost half of your body weight. All the movements you make, from blinking to running, depend on the action of muscles.

The muscles you will be most aware of are the big ones that you use to move your arms and legs about. These are the "voluntary" type of muscle which you can use whenever you want to—they are under your control. You use the large biceps muscle at the front of the upper arm, for example, to flex your arm—that is, to pull your hand up to your shoulder. It is also the muscle you use to demonstrate how strong you are!

But there are other, tiny muscles everywhere that do smaller but still crucial jobs inside the body. You use the muscles in your face to smile with, the muscles in your tongue to lick and speak with. Blinking muscles in the eyelids protect your eyes, and muscles around the lens of the eye let it focus. All these muscles are found near the surface of the body.

Inside your body are other muscles that mostly work of their own accord: these are known as involuntary muscles. Muscles in the wall of your gut push food through your intestines; without their action you could not digest your food. Other important muscles make up the walls of the heart and enable it to beat.

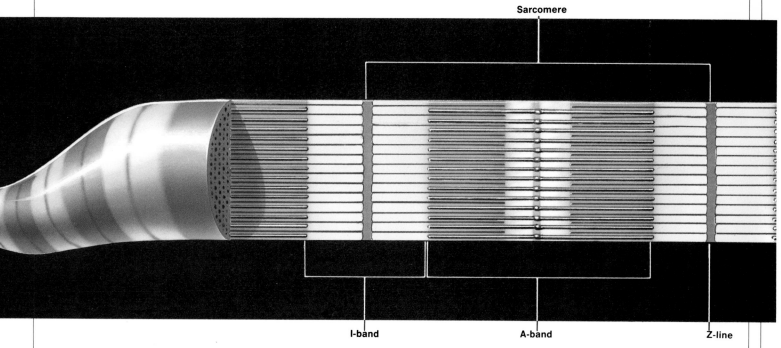

Sarcomere

I-band

A-band

Z-line

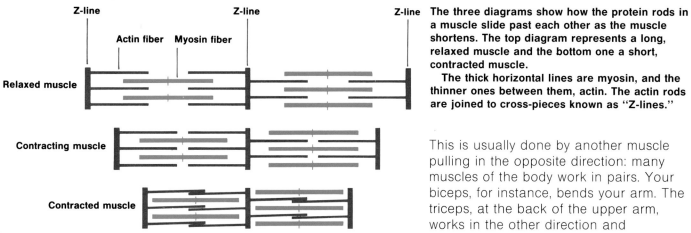

Z-line   Z-line   Z-line

Actin fiber   Myosin fiber

Relaxed muscle

Contracting muscle

Contracted muscle

The three diagrams show how the protein rods in a muscle slide past each other as the muscle shortens. The top diagram represents a long, relaxed muscle and the bottom one a short, contracted muscle.

The thick horizontal lines are myosin, and the thinner ones between them, actin. The actin rods are joined to cross-pieces known as "Z-lines."

28

How do muscles work?

Muscles work by contracting, that is, by getting shorter and thicker.

All animals, large and small, use muscles for moving themselves around or changing their shapes. It is muscles that let a jellyfish swim, a worm burrow, a sparrow fly or a person walk. In order to create movement, most muscles are joined at each end to something solid, like a bone, and this is pulled as the muscle gets shorter.

Muscles cannot make themselves longer. They can only shorten. This means that something has to pull them out to their full length again after they contract.

This is usually done by another muscle pulling in the opposite direction: many muscles of the body work in pairs. Your biceps, for instance, bends your arm. The triceps, at the back of the upper arm, works in the other direction and straightens the arm again.

To shorten, muscles need a great deal of energy. Energy is brought to them in the blood, mostly in the form of sugars like glucose. Muscles also need to be "told" to contract. This is done by a message brought by a nerve.

Inside each muscle cell there are two sets of thin rods which partly overlap. One set is made of a protein called myosin, the other of a different protein called actin. When supplied with energy and "switched on" by a nerve, the sets of rods slide past each other, making the muscle cell shorter and fatter as they overlap more and more.

When all the muscle cells do this together, the muscle contracts. While the muscle lengthens again, the rods slide back to their original positions.

29

How do I move my arms and legs?

When we walk, run or shake somebody by the hand, we control these movements by patterns of nerve messages. These messages are nerve impulses that start in the brain, when you "think" you want to do something.

The brain's messages are carried along nerves in the body until they reach the individual cells in muscles. Rapidly repeating signals tell the muscle it must contract.

The impulses enter the muscles at structures like miniature plugs. Inside these plugs the nerve impulses release a chemical substance called acetylcholine, which makes the muscle contract.

For proper coordinated movements of legs and arms, such as those you need to walk properly, the contractions must happen with perfect timing in several muscles at the same time.

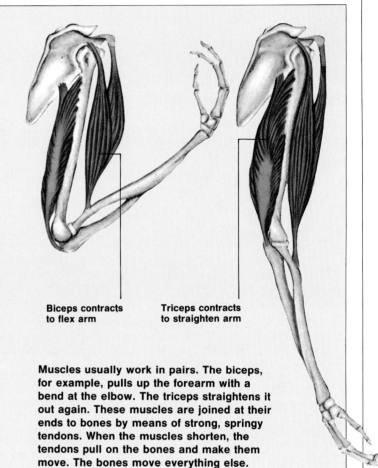

Biceps contracts to flex arm

Triceps contracts to straighten arm

Muscles usually work in pairs. The biceps, for example, pulls up the forearm with a bend at the elbow. The triceps straightens it out again. These muscles are joined at their ends to bones by means of strong, springy tendons. When the muscles shorten, the tendons pull on the bones and make them move. The bones move everything else.

30

Why do I get a stitch when I run?

A stitch is a sudden painful cramp in the muscles of your diaphragm. The diaphragm is the large dome of muscles that stretches inside your body, under your ribs and between your chest and your abdomen; it is used in breathing.

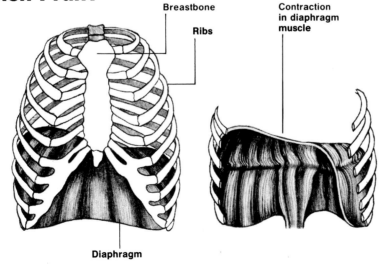

Breastbone

Ribs

Contraction in diaphragm muscle

Diaphragm

A stitch often comes when you suddenly start to exercise hard. This makes you begin breathing more quickly. A sudden demand for extra muscle activity like this can bring on a stitch. Bending over and reaching for the toes usually stretches the muscle enough to relieve the cramp.

The diaphragm muscles are not the only ones in which you can get cramps. They are particularly common in the calf muscles of the lower leg.

Some cramps are caused by lack of body salt, a problem which may arise in hot climates where the body can lose a lot of salt in sweat. Other cramps happen when the muscles do not get enough blood. One reason you should not swim after a meal is because a lot of blood is needed for digestion. Active muscles, starved of blood, can go into cramps.

The diaphragm stretches across the bottom of the ribcage. When a stitch occurs, the muscles in part of the diaphragm go into a painful contraction.

Why do some people have such big muscles?

Large muscles are partly inherited and partly something you can alter by your own lifestyle. In basic height and body shape you are somewhat like your parents, and your muscular build is partly inherited too. You are born of a light or a heavy build, or somewhere in between.

However, diet and exercise can change your final shape considerably. People with large muscles are usually well nourished but also regularly exercise their muscles hard. This exercise may be due to repetitive manual work—you do not see many puny lumberjacks, for instance.

In recent years, big muscles are also likely to be developed through regular training. This is usually based on some sort of controlled lifting or pulling of weights, using different parts of the body, in a gym or fitness center.

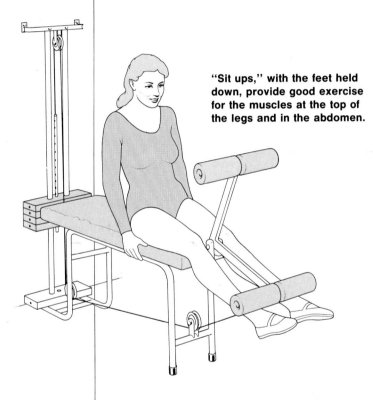

"Sit ups," with the feet held down, provide good exercise for the muscles at the top of the legs and in the abdomen.

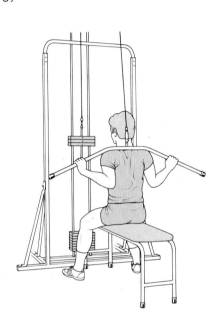

"Pull downs" on an exercise machine work the muscles of the arms, shoulders and neck.

"Push ups," from a lying position and against weights, strengthen arm and shoulder muscles.

32

What is blood made of?

By your late teens your body contains about seven pints (four liters) of blood, and most of it is water. But suspended and dissolved in that water is an incredibly varied mixture of cells and substances that help to make the blood the very useful liquid that it is.

Blood is alive: it contains living cells –

Different types of white blood cell

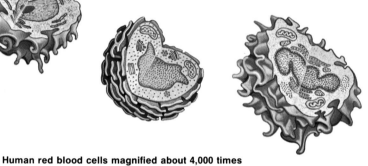

some red and others white. The liquid in which the red and white blood cells float is called plasma. Dissolved in the plasma are thousands of different materials. The most important ones include antibodies, "messengers" called hormones, foods such as glucose for energy, and waste substances.

White blood cells come in a number of different types, but all are involved in the body's defense system against disease. Some make protective antibodies; others engulf and eat bacteria.

Human red blood cells magnified about 4,000 times

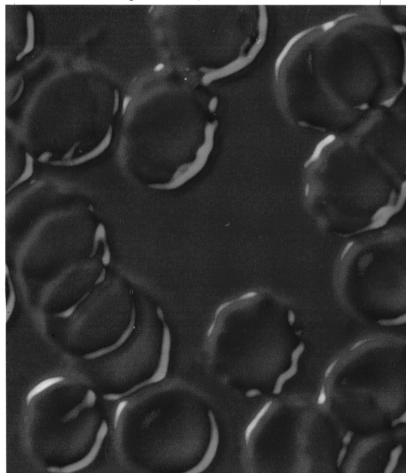

33

Why is blood red?

In every drop of your blood, there are many millions of red blood cells and it is these that make your blood red. Why are the cells themselves red? They contain large amounts of protein called hemoglobin which is bright red in color.

Hemoglobin contains iron, which helps this protein to be a very efficient carrier of oxygen, the gas that is needed by all the cells in your body to help keep you alive.

Oxygen from the air can stick on to the hemoglobin in red blood cells as they pass through the lungs. In the tissues of the body, the oxygen splits off from the hemoglobin and is used up.

In addition to the red blood cells are a number of different types of white blood cells, all concerned with protecting the body against invading germs.

How does blood get to my fingers and toes?

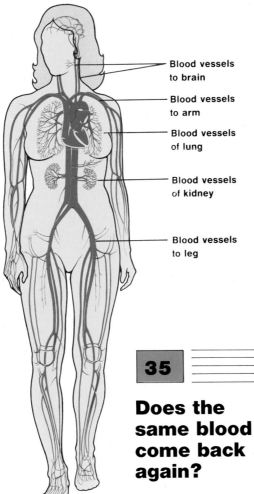

- Blood vessels to brain
- Blood vessels to arm
- Blood vessels of lung
- Blood vessels of kidney
- Blood vessels to leg

Blood gets to nearly every part of the body, including fingers and toes, in tubes or blood vessels called arteries. An artery is a blood vessel leading away from the heart, and blood is pumped into the arteries from the heart. All arteries have very smooth inside walls so the blood in them can flow along easily.

There is one main artery, called the dorsal aorta, leaving the heart. This artery divides, divides and divides again. This massive amount of branching means that every part of your body has its own arteries bringing the blood it needs. There are main arteries to the head, the arms, the gut, the liver, the kidneys and the legs.

Only a few parts of the body can manage without a blood supply: one is the transparent cornea of the eye.

Does the same blood come back again?

Yes, it does. As your heart pulses, it pushes the same blood back to any spot, time and time again. As the cells in the blood get worn out and die (each red blood cell lives for about 120 days), they are replaced by new ones, but the blood itself is not remade all the time.

The blood flows round the body in a circle from the heart, to the various organs, and back to the heart again. This means that there have to be connections between the arteries, which take blood from the heart, and the veins, which bring it back. In all organs the connections are very thin blood vessels called capillaries. They are so narrow that microscopic red blood cells pass down them in single file!

All organs have a mesh of narrow capillaries that join arteries to veins. It is within this branching network that the really useful work is done – providing oxygen and food for the tissues and picking up wastes. To do this the capillaries with their cargo of blood have to touch the cells of the body.

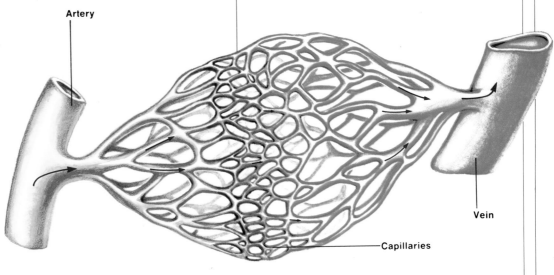

Artery

Vein

Capillaries

36

Why do the veins in my skin look blue?

All blood is red, and the veins are simply tubes, or vessels, full of blood. But the reason that the veins, such as those on the inside of your wrist or the back of your hand, look blue is related to one of the main jobs blood does—carrying oxygen to all parts of the body.

Red blood cells can do this job because they contain the oxygen-carrying protein called hemoglobin, which is red. At least— it is red when it is carrying oxygen, because oxygen and hemoglobin link up to form the substance oxy-hemoglobin which is a really bright red. Blood coming from the lungs loaded with oxygen is

therefore bright red in color.

Blood is still bright red when it is being pushed around the body, in strong tubes known as arteries. But when it has given up its oxygen to the body's tissues it needs to return to the lungs to get some more. The veins are the blood vessels taking this stale or "de-oxygenated" blood back to the heart before going back to the lungs.

The hemoglobin in blood that has lost its oxygen is blue-red or purplish in color, not bright red any more. It looks blue because the veins have thinner walls than arteries and the blood shows through.

37

Is everyone's blood the same?

Everyone's blood contains water, salts, red blood cells, white blood cells, dissolved food and hormones (chemical messengers). Your blood has these whether you are young or old, female or male and wherever you were born.

But every person is an individual: your own combination of genes makes you

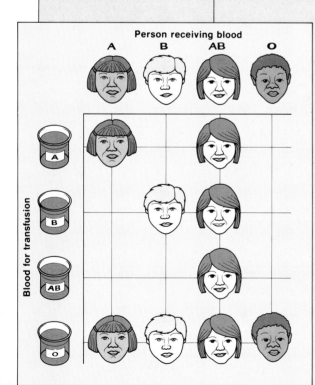

Blood transfusions have to be carried out with great care so that the body does not "reject" the new blood being given.

Four blood groups are especially important. They are called A, B, AB and O. These letters are used to refer to the molecules dotted on the surface of the red cells.

Group A blood has type A molecules; Group B has type B molecules; Group AB has both and Group O has neither. Group A will reject Group B and Group B will reject Group A. Group AB rejects nothing and Group O rejects all types except other O blood. The chart on the left shows which transfusions are possible.

different from any other person that has ever lived (unless you happen to be one of a pair of identical twins!). Part of this uniqueness is the fact that there are some detailed differences between one person's blood and another's.

The differences can only be seen when your blood is analyzed carefully by examining it under a microscope and doing tests on it. These differences are important for blood transfusions, where a person who has lost a lot of blood is given another person's blood, and for transplant surgery, where someone is given another person's organ.

Unless the new blood or organ is from a person with blood that is very similar in every way, the body's defensive system will swing into action to reject it. Recognizing the blood as foreign, the defenses of the person receiving the transfusion or transplant will attack the new blood. If this happens, the person may become very ill and could die.

Blood has been classified into different types or groups since the beginning of this century, when the Austrian Nobel prize-winner Karl Landsteiner worked out the broad differences between them. He also found out which blood types could be swapped so that patients always get blood which their bodies will accept. Before that, safe blood transfusions were impossible.

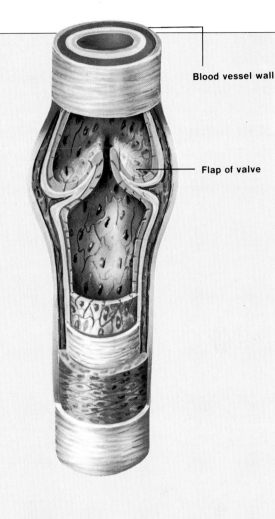

Blood vessel wall

Flap of valve

38

How can blood flow up your legs?

Blood returning to the heart from veins in the feet, legs and abdomen has to flow uphill. So does blood leaving the heart to supply the upper part of the chest, the arms, and the head. It can do this because it is in closed tubes, known as veins and arteries, and is being pushed along by a powerful pump—the heart. The heart pushes blood into the arteries and continues pushing even when blood is returning in the veins. It is rather like the water in a central heating system being pushed through pipes from a boiler and pump on the first floor of a house into radiators on the second floor.

The main arteries of your body have strong, elastic walls to cope with the powerful surge of oxygen-rich blood that happens as the heart beats. Once the arteries have carried the blood to all the different parts of your body, and delivered oxygen to the tissues, the stale blood is returned to the heart along the veins. The veins have thinner walls since the stale blood no longer moves in such powerful surges. Some veins even have one-way valves, to make sure the blood keeps flowing in the right direction, and does not stop or flow backward.

To help stop back-flow in the slowest parts of the blood's uphill journey, many veins have valves in them. These are internal flaps that let blood flow in the right direction (up to the heart) but stop it flowing backward.

Valve open

Valve closed

39

Why don't I bleed to death when I cut myself?

Because your blood is vital for life, your body has a number of "failsafe" mechanisms which ensure that you do not lose too much blood from a broken blood vessel if you cut yourself.

You bleed when a blood-carrying vessel gets damaged. When this happens the vessel tries to shut itself off. Unlike a burst water pipe, which could not shut off the water supply, the body manages this trick because the blood vessels have a sleeve of muscle around them. When blood vessels are damaged, these muscles contract so as to squeeze them until the blood flow slows down or stops.

The blood itself has another safety feature. When exposed to air, blood clots: it changes from a liquid to a solid, in other words it "sets." This clotting plugs holes in broken blood vessels.

40

Is my heart heart-shaped?

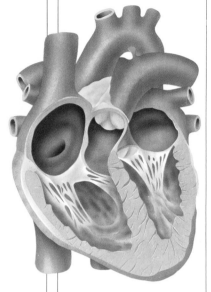

The symbolic heart with an arrow through it is only roughly the shape of a real heart. As the picture shows, the heart that actually beats inside you is shaped more like an upside-down pear.

The heart has four blood-filled spaces inside it. The two atria form the double domes at the top and the two ventricles form the pointed base, both of which are "correctly" drawn on the graphic heart.

The upper side of the heart is covered with large blood vessels that join on to the different parts of the heart. These vessels carry blood to and from the heart as it beats. The thick-walled blood vessels that carry blood away from the heart are called arteries. Thinner-walled ones that return blood from the body to the heart are known as the veins.

41

How big is it?

The heart is surprisingly small considering the crucial job it does. Sandwiched between the lungs and the middle of the chest, it is about the size of a clenched fist. Even in an adult it only weighs about 11 ounces (310 grams).

The heart fits into its own lubricated chamber, the pericardial cavity, which enables it to beat freely. It is surrounded by the protective ribcage and has the diaphragm, a tough sheet of muscle, below it.

Doctors can judge the size of a heart accurately by X-raying it or doing a whole-body scan. A larger than normal heart can sometimes be a clue to heart or lung disease – a heart that is too big may be having to work excessively hard.

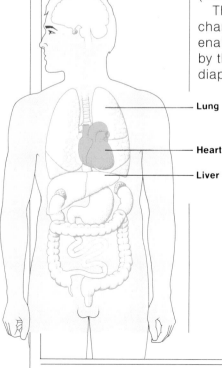

Lung

Heart

Liver

The heart is placed above the diaphragm and between the lungs. The diagram shows how small the heart is in relation to the lungs and the liver, for example.

42

Why does my heart beat?

The heart is a never-failing pumping organ that pushes blood around the body, from the time you are a baby-to-be inside your mother until the moment you die.

Your body needs this pumped supply of blood because it does two vital jobs. First, it brings food and oxygen (the gas you need to stay alive) to all the tissues of the body. Second, and at the same time, it removes poisonous wastes from those same parts. These two life-supporting jobs must be carried on constantly for life to continue.

1. Blood returns to both atria from the lungs and the rest of the body.

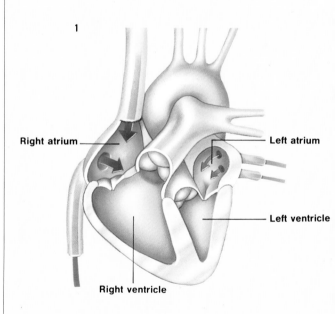

1

Right atrium

Left atrium

Left ventricle

Right ventricle

The trace (right) is an electrocardiogram (EKG) which records the electrical activity of the heart. Tall spikes show the ventricles contracting. Doctors use changes or "faults" in the trace to help them detect heart disease.

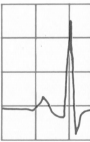

Around 70 to 80 times a minute, and even more often in babies and young children, a heart beats inside the chest. A matching pulse can be felt at the neck or wrist in time with the heart beats. The pulse is the surge of blood in the arteries that follows each squeeze of the heart's muscular pump.

So vital is the beating of the heart, that if a doctor needs to carry out surgery on the heart, the patient has to be connected up to a heart-lung machine first. Only in this way, with the machine keeping the flow of oxygen-containing blood going, can the surgeon stop the heart in order to operate.

How does it do this?

The heart is a pump made of muscles of a special sort. These cardiac muscles can pulsate – first contracting, then relaxing, without your having to think about it. As they do so, they squeeze blood through spaces in the heart.

The squeezing rate of the heart is automatically regulated by nerves. These ensure that it speeds up when you need extra blood – for instance, when you run – and slows down when you're asleep.

The heart has four chambers, two on the left side and two on the right. Each joined-up pair of chambers consists of an upper atrium into which blood flows, and a lower ventricle which pushes blood out again.

The two pairs of pumping organs are needed because the heart supplies two circulations. One passes through the lungs, where blood picks up oxygen from the air. The other takes oxygen-rich blood around the rest of the body. The right ventricle pushes blood into the lungs while the left supplies the other body organs.

The four drawings below show what happens as the heart pumps during a single beat.

2. Both atria contract at the same time, pushing blood through valves into the two ventricles.

3. Both ventricles contract powerfully, sending blood to the lungs and around the body.

4. The heart returns to its first state (1), ready for the next beat.

2
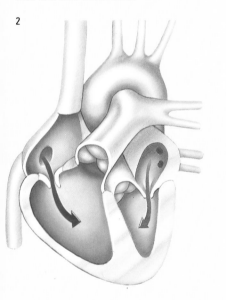

3
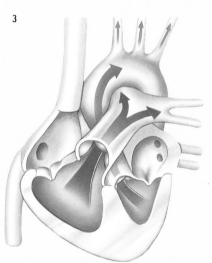
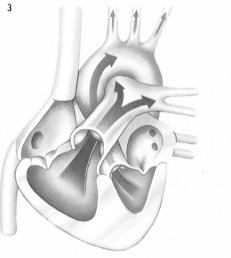

4
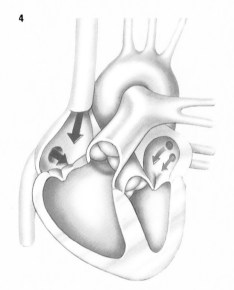

Why do people jog to keep fit?

Jogging has become an increasingly popular form of exercise in the last ten to twenty years. It is an easy and convenient way of keeping fit: you don't need a gym or special equipment and you can jog whenever it suits you.

Like swimming, rope skipping, cycling and dancing, jogging is an aerobic exercise. That means the body takes and uses more oxygen while the exercise is being performed. (Sprinting, in contrast, is anaerobic—no extra oxygen is taken in as it is done.)

The body's aerobic system is that which carries oxygen from the air into the muscle fibers. Working muscles (as in jogging) need extra oxygen, so the lungs are encouraged to take in more than usual. All forms of aerobic exercise make you a little breathless and therefore force you to breathe harder. So they improve the efficiency of your body's oxygen delivery system, and the way in which your muscles produce energy.

Steady, slow-to-medium speed running, over distances of more than a mile, is an easy and convenient form of aerobic exercise. Jogging regularly allows you to make the best possible use of your lungs.

Jogging is also good for your heart. It speeds up your heart rate and increases its pumping power. There is good evidence that exercise like this reduces the risk of heart disease in later life, as well as making you feel toned up and generally fitter and healthier.

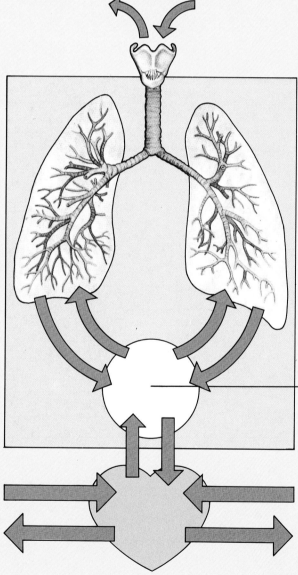

Air in and out of lungs

Oxygen exchange in air sacs (alveoli)

Blood flow from heart to and from body and lungs

The heart and lungs are exercised well through jogging. As you jog, your breathing rate and heart rate both increase, exercising your heart and lungs at the same time as your leg muscles.

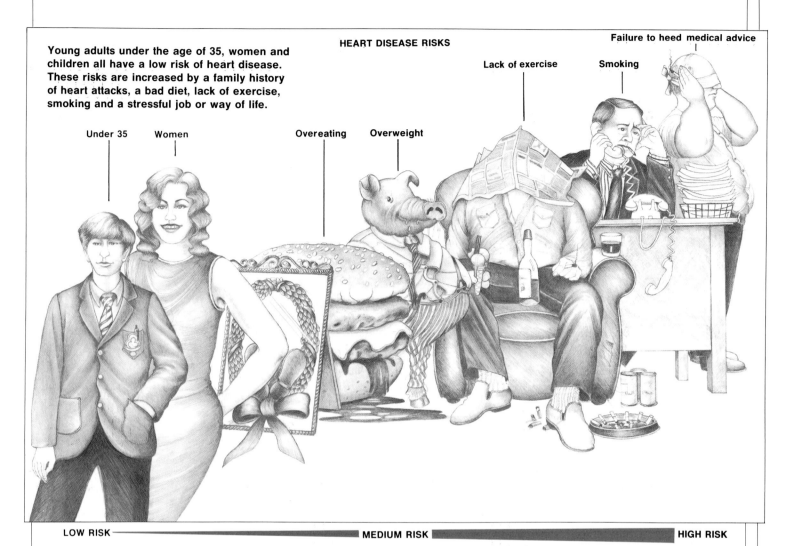

HEART DISEASE RISKS

Young adults under the age of 35, women and children all have a low risk of heart disease. These risks are increased by a family history of heart attacks, a bad diet, lack of exercise, smoking and a stressful job or way of life.

Under 35   Women   Overeating   Overweight   Lack of exercise   Smoking   Failure to heed medical advice

LOW RISK ———————————— MEDIUM RISK ————————————— HIGH RISK

45

What is a heart attack?

Heart disease is one of the commonest causes of death in the Western world. It shows up most dramatically in the form of heart attacks.

A heart attack is a sudden, painful "seizure" when part of the muscle of the heart stops working. This is a dangerous emergency. If a large part of the heart stops working for too long, a person will die, because blood will stop circulating around the body.

The most usual cause of a heart attack is a blockage in the blood supply to the heart itself. The muscles of the heart need their own supply of oxygenated blood in order to keep pumping, and they get it from blood that arrives in the heart's own coronary arteries. If these arteries become blocked anywhere, the part of heart muscle with a blocked supply cannot carry on working properly.

Blockage of the coronary arteries happens in older people if their arteries "fur up" inside. The narrowed artery is more easily blocked by a blood clot. The risks of this type of artery blockage are generally greater in men than in women and significantly greater in old people than young ones. But the tendency to heart attacks can be aggravated by the ways some people live, by their eating habits, and by the things they do.

Smoking, being overweight, eating a fatty diet, getting too little exercise and leading a stressful life all increase the risk of heart disease. Inherited factors also play a part. The best ways to cut down the risk are to get regular exercise, eat a healthy diet, watch your weight and never to smoke.

The small cutaway diagram of the whole heart shows the places where a baby's heart may fail to grow properly in its mother's womb. The risk areas are the wall between the left and right atria (A), the wall between the left and right ventricles (B), and the link (called the ductus arteriosus) between the artery to the lungs and the large artery called the dorsal aorta (C).

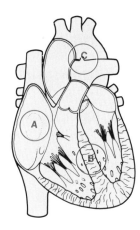

What is a blue baby?

Blue babies are babies who are born sick because their blood does not get enough oxygen. Blood without enough oxygen is bluish, hence the babies' unhealthy color.

The illness that causes the problems with the blood is usually the result of a mistake in the growth of the baby's heart within the mother's womb. In the case of blue babies, the error makes oxygen-carrying and stale blood without oxygen get mixed up in the heart.

In the normal heart, these two kinds of blood are kept well apart. In a blue baby, mixed blood is being sent around the body. So, instead of carrying large amounts of oxygen, the arteries have low-oxygen blood in them. This means that all parts of the body are starved of oxygen to a certain extent. The baby is weak, tired, and does not thrive.

The three main types of wrong heart growth all result in incorrect "pipework," causing dangerous blood mixing. The first type is a gap in the wall that should separate the two atria, or upper chambers of the heart. The second is a similar gap in the wall between the two ventricles, or lower chambers. These defects are often called "holes in the heart." The holes do not let blood out of the heart, but they allow stale blood on the right side of the heart to mix with oxygen-rich blood on the left.

The third problem is a dangerous join between the artery to the lungs and the main artery to the body. This also lets the two kinds of blood which should be separate become mixed. These problems can usually be cured by heart surgery.

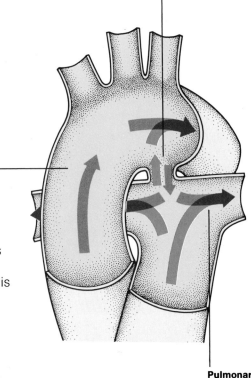

The large diagram (above right) shows an open ductus arteriosus. This link between the main blood supply to the lungs and the body should close off with a baby's first breath. If it stays open, stale blood, low in oxygen, gets passed around the body.

The diagram (right) shows how the same danger arises if the holes in the walls between either atria or ventricles of the heart stay open after the birth. Like the ductus arteriosus, these two blood routes should close off when the baby is born.

Ductus arteriosus

Dorsal aorta

Pulmonary artery

Hole between ventricles

Hole between atria

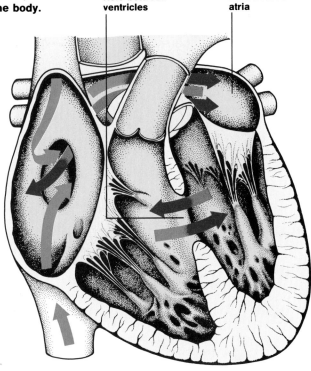

47

What is a heart transplant?

A heart transplant consists of taking the entire heart from a person who has just died and replacing the patient's faulty heart with this new one. This is possible because the muscles of the heart stay alive for a few hours after a person dies.

There are some types of heart disease that are so serious they cannot be cured by either medicines or normal surgery. Before 1967, when the South African surgeon Christiaan Barnard carried out the first human heart transplant, no other course of treatment was possible. A heart transplant is, however, a dangerous treatment of last resort, and may only lengthen a person's life a little.

The transplant operation is a difficult one because of the number of blood vessels that have to be correctly connected up. While this is going on, the patient must be kept alive on a heart-lung machine, which does the work of both heart and lungs.

More difficult than this, though, is stopping the patient "rejecting" the new heart. Special drugs have to be used to try to stop the body from attacking the transplant because it is "foreign." Even with these, though, rejection usually occurs eventually.

48

Can you make a new heart?

No. But research scientists and surgeons in the United States have been trying for some time to make an artificial heart.

The idea for such a heart at the moment is not one that would be placed permanently in the chest like the transplanted heart in a transplant operation. It is instead being designed to keep a patient alive for a short time (perhaps a few days) after his or her own heart stops working. This period might give just enough time for a dead donor to be found which would enable a heart transplant to take place.

The "Jarvic 7" artificial heart consists of two plastic pumps made out of an aluminum frame and tubes of a plastic called Dacron. The pumps take over the blood-pushing action of the heart. One of the big problems is the power source—how can the pumps be made to work?

In the Jarvic 7 heart the power comes from outside of the body via compressed air pipes. These are used to inflate the diaphragms, the parts of the pumps that push the blood out. As well as all the other problems of design, these air pipes have to enter the chest and present a serious infection risk.

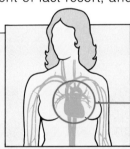

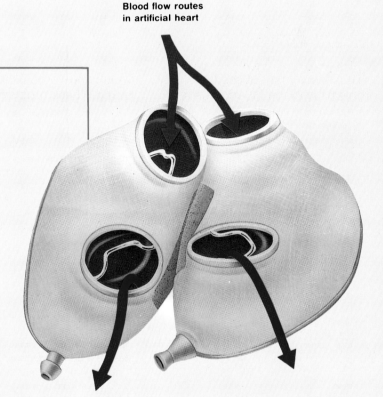

Blood flow routes in artificial heart

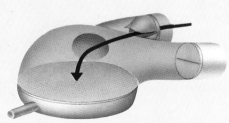

Diaphragm down (blood pulled in)

Diaphragm up (blood pushed out)

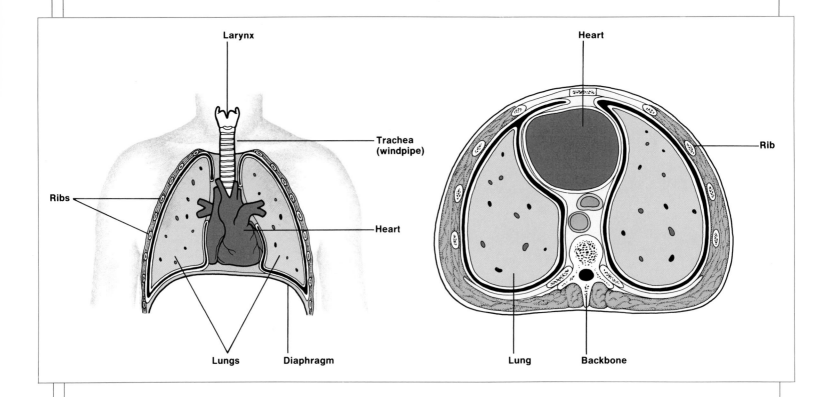

Larynx

Trachea (windpipe)

Ribs

Heart

Lungs

Diaphragm

Heart

Rib

Lung

Backbone

Why do we breathe?

We breathe in order to get the life-supporting gas called oxygen into our bodies. We need a continual supply of oxygen for energy and our bodies are constantly using it up. If the supply of oxygen ran out for just a short time, we would die.

This vital need for oxygen is something that people have in common with most other animals. All these living creatures use oxygen in a very efficient way to produce energy.

After it gets inside your body, oxygen is carried to your body's cells in blood, where it dissolves in the liquids inside them. Here it is used in a process called "internal respiration." In this, the oxygen is used to "burn" sugars like glucose, also present in your cells. The burning, which happens at normal temperatures, releases large amounts of an energy-rich substance. At the same time, respiration creates two waste products—the gas, carbon dioxide, and water. Carbon dioxide waste is breathed out.

So we breathe in to take oxygen from the atmosphere into our lungs. We breathe out and remove carbon dioxide from our bodies.

The lungs, shown above left in cutaway front view, are large, spongy organs located in the chest. They are the organs in which oxygen enters the body and by which carbon dioxide leaves it.

This cross-section through the middle of the chest (above) shows the position of the two lungs in relation to the heart and the surrounding ribs.

Do we all breathe at the same rate?

People's breathing rates alter according to what they are doing. Gentle breathing while you are asleep may be at the rate of about 12–14 breaths a minute. If you are involved in strenuous exercise, your breathing rate may well be double that rate, or more. Young babies, however, breathe even more quickly—at a rate of 33–40 breaths per minute.

If you are ill and have a raised body temperature, you almost always breathe faster as well. This is why patient charts in hospitals record your temperature and your breathing rate at regular intervals. Both are useful in checking a patient's progress.

Different animals also breathe at different rates. Warm-blooded animals and those which are highly active tend to breathe faster than cold-blooded animals or those with sluggish lifestyles.

These differences are tied up with the varying energy needs of the two types of animal. To take two extreme examples, a hovering hummingbird may take a breath once every second or even faster, while a hibernating hedgehog's breathing slows down so much it is hardly detectable. The hummingbird, with a body temperature of over 103 degrees Farenheit (40 degrees Celsius), has high energy needs, whereas the hedgehog, whose temperature during hibernation may drop to almost freezing point, has a very low energy need.

Does it make any difference whether I breathe in through my mouth or my nose?

A downward section through the head shows the air pathways to the windpipe via the nose and mouth.

Not really. The airspaces of the lungs are connected both to the back of your mouth and to the cavity inside your nose, via the trachea or windpipe.

You can breathe through your nose with your mouth shut, or through your mouth when your nose is blocked, for example with a cold. Or you can breathe through both together, especially when you need to take in extra air, as when you are running.

Breathing in through the nose is generally better, since the nose is lined with hairs that can filter out some of the dust particles in dirty air. The nose cavity also warms and moistens air before it gets to the lungs. Nose breathing is obviously useful when you are talking, or during eating, while there is food in your mouth. It is also how a baby breathes when sucking the breast or a bottle.

It is in fact rare that you think consciously about your breathing and the way you are doing it. Most of the time you do it quite automatically.

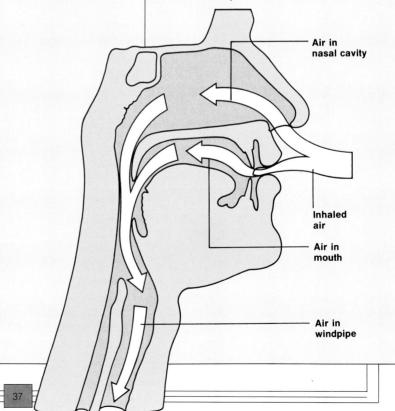

Air in
nasal cavity

Inhaled
air

Air in
mouth

Air in
windpipe

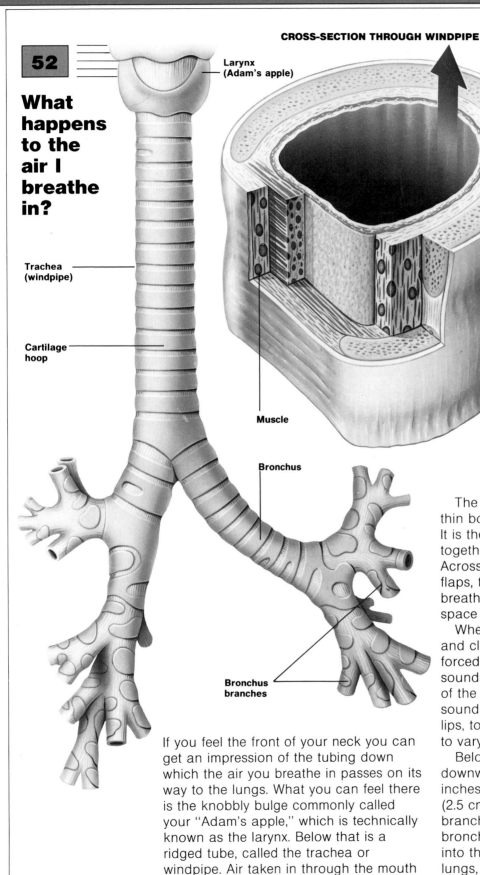

52

What happens to the air I breathe in?

Larynx
(Adam's apple)

Trachea
(windpipe)

Cartilage
hoop

Muscle

Bronchus

Bronchus
branches

Cartilage hoop

The airway tubing between the larynx and the lungs (far left) is ridged in appearance because both the windpipe and the bronchi are strengthened with hoops of cartilage. The hoops stop the airspace in the center of the windpipe from collapsing.

The cutaway view of a section of the windpipe (left) shows the position of a cartilage hoop in the windpipe wall, as well as the muscle layers in the wall itself.

If you feel the front of your neck you can get an impression of the tubing down which the air you breathe in passes on its way to the lungs. What you can feel there is the knobbly bulge commonly called your "Adam's apple," which is technically known as the larynx. Below that is a ridged tube, called the trachea or windpipe. Air taken in through the mouth or nose passes first through the larynx and then down the windpipe.

The larynx is a complicated structure of thin bone, cartilage (gristle) and muscles. It is the part of the body which, working together with the tongue, lets us speak. Across the center of the larynx stretch two flaps, the vocal cords. During ordinary breathing, they are relaxed, leaving a wide space for the air to pass through.

When we speak the cords become taut and closer together. They vibrate as air is forced past them, making the basic sounds of speech. Changing the tautness of the cords helps to alter the pitch of any sound that you are making. You use your lips, tongue and the shape of your mouth to vary the noises made in the larynx.

Below the larynx, the windpipe stretches downward to the lungs. It is about $4\frac{1}{2}$ inches (11 cm) long and up to an inch (2.5 cm) across. At its base, the windpipe branches into two stubby tubes, the bronchi, which are the airways leading into the left and right lungs. Within the lungs, the bronchi branch and branch again, like a tree, creating more and more, finer and finer, air tubing in the lungs.

How do I breathe in and out?

You breathe air in and out of your lungs by changing the shape of the chest cavity in which the two lungs sit.

This cavity, known as the pleural cavity, is protected by a bony "cage," the ribcage. The ribcage consists of the breastbone at the front, ribs curving from the breastbone around to the bones of the spine, and the backbone of the chest itself. The base of the cavity is formed by a tough muscle sheet, the diaphragm.

When you breathe in, muscles between your ribs work to lift the ribs upward and forward, expanding the size of the chest cavity inside your ribcage. At the same time the muscles of the diaphragm contract, flattening the dome. This two-fold expansion pulls air into the lungs within the enlarged cavity.

When both rib muscles and diaphragm muscles relax, the ribcage falls and the diaphragm domes up again. Together these two changes squeeze the chest cavity to a smaller size and air is forced out of the lungs.

The whole breathing operation, though it sounds strenuous, takes place smoothly and seemingly without effort. The lungs are covered with a thin, slippery membrane, separating them from the chest wall. This enables the lungs and ribcage to slide easily, without friction, during breathing.

When the ribcage expands upward and outward, and the diaphragm is pulled down, you breathe in. When the ribcage sinks and the diaphragm domes upward again, you breathe out.

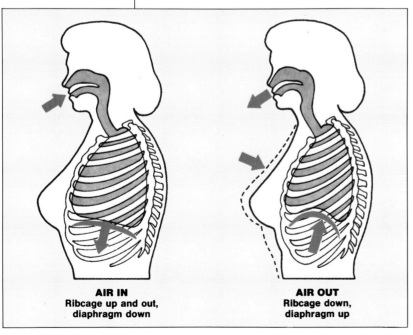

AIR IN
Ribcage up and out, diaphragm down

AIR OUT
Ribcage down, diaphragm up

How long can I hold my breath?

Usually for about a minute, but the world record, achieved on an underwater dive, is over five minutes!

Normally, the rhythm of breathing is quite automatic, with each outward breath following each breath taken in. If you breathe in and then deliberately hold your breath, you will find it increasingly difficult not to breathe out again.

Your brain has some very sensible safety devices that attempt to make you automatically breathe in again as the level of oxygen in your blood falls and that of carbon dioxide goes up. You have to fight those safety mechanisms to hold your breath and stop yourself from breathing out.

If you could somehow manage to keep holding your breath, you would eventually become unconscious. At that point, the brain would take over, like a sort of automatic pilot—and you would begin breathing again.

Why do I get breathless when I run?

The sensation of breathlessness is the feeling you get when your body is not getting sufficient oxygen, and not getting it fast enough. You feel you have "run out of breath," and your body reacts with an uncontrollable urge to try and breathe faster and deeper in order to take in more air.

When you run or get other strenuous exercise, your muscles are working hard. This means you need more energy, so you use up oxygen more quickly than normal. You therefore need to get air into your lungs faster to keep up with this demand. The brain reflexes automatically speed up your breathing to match the supply of oxygen breathed in with the demands of the body.

How do my lungs work?

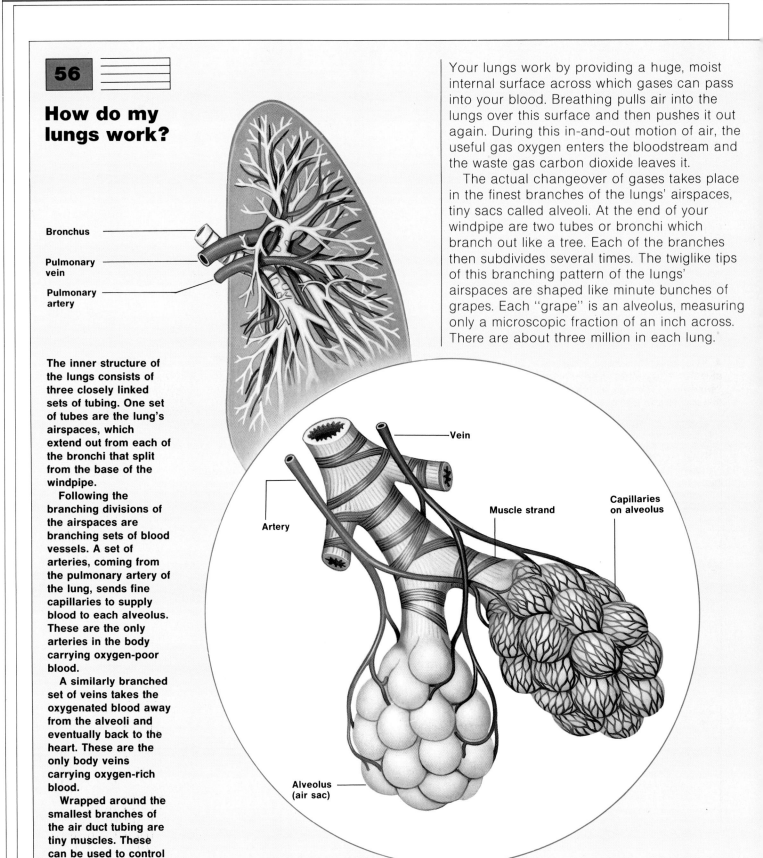

Bronchus

Pulmonary vein

Pulmonary artery

Vein

Artery

Muscle strand

Capillaries on alveolus

Alveolus (air sac)

The inner structure of the lungs consists of three closely linked sets of tubing. One set of tubes are the lung's airspaces, which extend out from each of the bronchi that split from the base of the windpipe.

Following the branching divisions of the airspaces are branching sets of blood vessels. A set of arteries, coming from the pulmonary artery of the lung, sends fine capillaries to supply blood to each alveolus. These are the only arteries in the body carrying oxygen-poor blood.

A similarly branched set of veins takes the oxygenated blood away from the alveoli and eventually back to the heart. These are the only body veins carrying oxygen-rich blood.

Wrapped around the smallest branches of the air duct tubing are tiny muscles. These can be used to control the size of the total airspace of the lung.

Your lungs work by providing a huge, moist internal surface across which gases can pass into your blood. Breathing pulls air into the lungs over this surface and then pushes it out again. During this in-and-out motion of air, the useful gas oxygen enters the bloodstream and the waste gas carbon dioxide leaves it.

The actual changeover of gases takes place in the finest branches of the lungs' airspaces, tiny sacs called alveoli. At the end of your windpipe are two tubes or bronchi which branch out like a tree. Each of the branches then subdivides several times. The twiglike tips of this branching pattern of the lungs' airspaces are shaped like minute bunches of grapes. Each "grape" is an alveolus, measuring only a microscopic fraction of an inch across. There are about three million in each lung.

When you breathe in, air reaches the space inside of each alveolus. Here it is separated from the blood in your capillaries (the tiniest blood vessels) by only a very thin membrane, or skinlike sheet. Gases pass easily through this membrane by a process called diffusion.

Diffusion means that each gas travels "downhill" from a region where there is a lot of it to a region where there is less. There is more oxygen in the air than in the blood of the lung capillaries, so oxygen passes into the blood there. And since there is more carbon dioxide in the blood than in the air of the alveolus, this waste gas diffuses out into the airspace.

So diffusion takes place in both directions at once in each alveolus, to make sure that your body gets the oxygen it needs and, at the same time, gets rid of the poisonous carbon dioxide.

A highly magnified section through a lung alveolus shows the thin membrane "sandwich" between air and blood. It is across this membrane that gases diffuse.

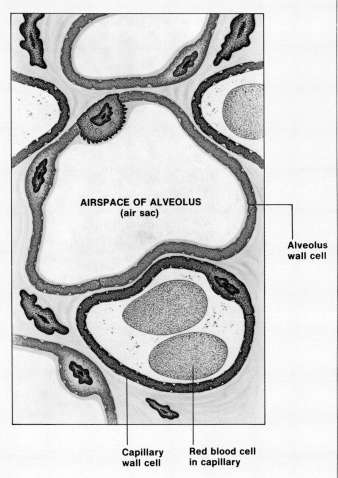

AIRSPACE OF ALVEOLUS
(air sac)

Alveolus
wall cell

Capillary
wall cell

Red blood cell
in capillary

How does oxygen get from my lungs to the rest of my body?

The oxygen travels in your blood. Getting oxygen into the bloodstream and transporting it around the body is such a crucial task that half the heart has the job of supplying the lungs with blood. The other half of the heart takes care of the rest of the body. As the heart beats, it pumps blood into two separate circulation systems, shown below.

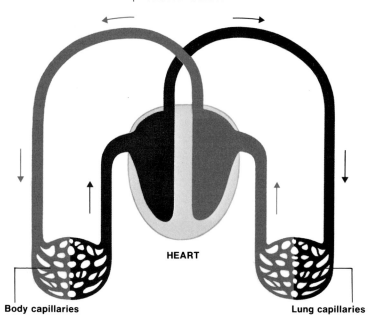

HEART

Body capillaries   Lung capillaries

Red = oxygenated blood   Black = deoxygenated blood

The above diagram shows the "plumbing" arrangements of blood between your heart and lungs which allow oxygen to reach the rest of your body.

The heart is really two, two-chambered pumps. The ventricles on each side of the heart pump blood out into the arteries. The right ventricle sends blood to both lungs along the pulmonary arteries. Blood with high oxygen levels returns from the lungs to the left atrium of the heart, which passes it on to the left ventricle. This then forces this oxygen-rich stream around all the rest of your body.

Once the left ventricle of the heart receives oxygenated blood from the lungs, it pumps this blood out into the dorsal aorta, the main artery from the heart. The blood in this "systemic" circulation is pumped out from the heart under high pressure to enable it to reach all parts of the body. In the "pulmonary," or lung, circulation, stale or deoxygenated blood is pumped from the heart to the lungs under lower pressure. The blood then picks up more oxygen in the lungs and the cycle continues.

The oxygen in the blood is carried in two ways. Some is simply dissolved in the liquid part of blood. Most, though, is carried attached to the red pigment, hemoglobin, found inside red blood cells.

What does cigarette smoking do to your lungs?

Smoking cigarettes stops your lungs working efficiently. It also causes several unpleasant diseases of the lungs and heart, the worst being lung cancer. Cigarette smoking is a thoroughly dangerous and unhealthy activity. It damages not only smokers but also the people around them who are forced to breathe in their tobacco smoke.

The harmful changes come about because your lungs cannot cope with large quantities of poisonous substances that pass into them if you are a regular smoker. The most important poisons in tobacco smoke are the gas carbon monoxide, smoke particles, nicotine and tar substances.

The poisons make the lungs produce a lot of mucus and they also stop that mucus being cleared from the lungs. Most of the air tubing of the lungs is lined with a carpet of cells carrying microscopic hairs that beat to-and-fro, moving mucus, dust and other particles out of the lungs. In smokers, an excessive amount of mucus stops these hairs, called cilia, from working efficiently, so the lungs clog up. Clogged lungs are liable to become infected, producing the disease bronchitis.

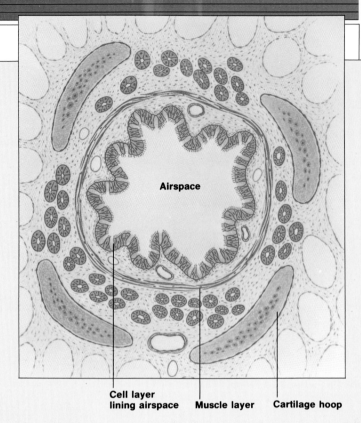

Airspace

Cell layer lining airspace   Muscle layer   Cartilage hoop

Long-term smoking finally destroys the tiny air sacs in the lungs, and makes the air passages close down. The worst disease caused by smoking is lung cancer, which causes great suffering and finally kills. Most lung cancer is started by the cancer-causing poisons contained in cigarette smoke.

If after reading this you still want to smoke, you cannot say you have not been warned!

Why does the doctor listen to my chest with a stethoscope?

A stethoscope is simply a device that magnifies the sounds coming from inside your body, so helping a doctor to identify them. It consists of a funnel with a membrane that is placed on your skin, and some carefully shaped tubing that can carry sounds to the doctor's ears. Sounds made by the lungs and heart as they work can give detailed clues about what might be wrong with these organs.

Doctors move the stethoscope around the front and back of your chest to hear noises in all parts of both left and right lungs. In healthy lungs, all they can hear is a quiet moving in and out of air. In diseased lungs there may be added sounds. The commonest are "wheezes," "crackles," and "rubs." Wheezing noises happen in diseases such as asthma and smoking damage, and are caused by narrowed-down air tubes with too much mucus in them. Crackles are moist sounds, often at the bottom of the lungs, which happen in infections like pneumonia. If the crackle disappears when the doctor asks you to cough, it is probably only due to a little mucus in the larger tubes, and is not serious.

Creaky "rubbing" sounds occur in pleurisy, a serious disease in which the tissue membranes surrounding the lungs become infected. The inflamed membranes rub against each other.

Normal heart sounds heard with a stethoscope are the "lub-dub" noises of the valves inside the heart closing during the heart beat. "Murmurs" are the worrying noises heard when the valves are not operating properly, or when there are abnormal holes in heart walls.

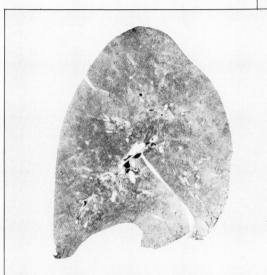

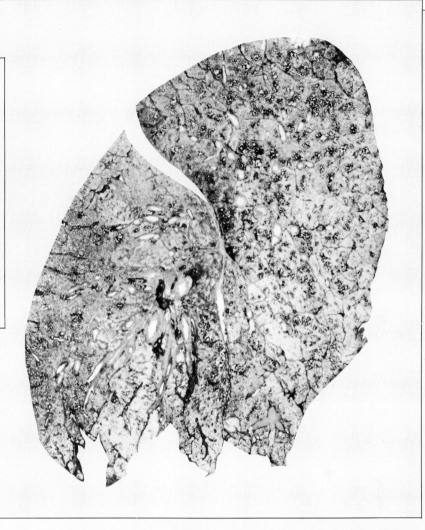

A section through a healthy lung (above) shows smooth foamy tissue, a mixture of fine air tubes and clusters of tiny air sacs (alveoli).

In a lung damaged by cigarette smoking (right), the smooth foamy appearance is altered in a sinister manner. Dark clusters of accumulated tar deposits can be seen, and tough, fibrous material, laid down by the lungs in an attempt to protect themselves, changes the smooth appearance of the tissues.

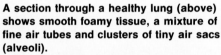

Can breathing polluted air damage your lungs?

It depends on the type of polluted air being breathed. Some types of dirty air are extremely dangerous and can certainly damage lung tissue, sometimes in a way that cannot be treated or cured successfully. Other types of pollution only cause temporary problems and do not actually damage the lungs permanently.

The commonest type of polluted air that is breathed is cigarette smoke, and that most certainly damages your lungs and possibly your heart too. The other dangerous types are much less common. They tend to occur mainly from particular dirty jobs that workers have to carry out, particularly if they do not wear a proper mask, or breathing apparatus to protect themselves.

Coal miners and quarry workers can have their lungs badly damaged by breathing in rock or coal dust over many years. This dust accumulates in the lungs as dark deposits, and this foreign matter causes the lungs to produce tough, fibrous tissue in an attempt to "wrap up" the invading dust. This tissue can stop the lungs working at their full efficiency which restricts the body's ability to exercise.

Asbestos dust is perhaps the most feared mineral dust. Minute asbestos fibers breathed into the lungs can produce damaging changes to the lungs themselves and to the membranes around them. In some people whose lungs are contaminated with asbestos, a rare form of lung cancer is started by this pollution.

Where does food go after I've eaten it?

The gut is an enormously long and complicated tube, stretching from your mouth to your anus. It serves as a passageway for food. During its journey, the food is digested and its useful parts absorbed by your body.

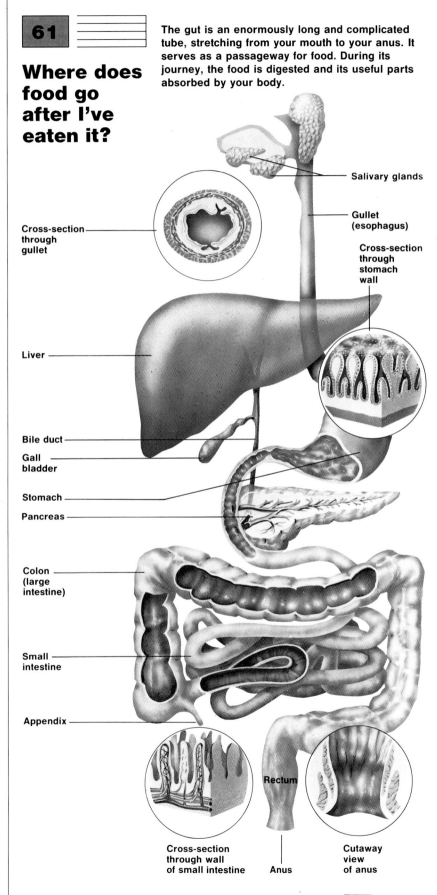

Salivary glands

Gullet (esophagus)

Cross-section through gullet

Cross-section through stomach wall

Liver

Bile duct

Gall bladder

Stomach

Pancreas

Colon (large intestine)

Small intestine

Appendix

Rectum

Cross-section through wall of small intestine

Anus

Cutaway view of anus

Once you have put food or drink into your mouth, it starts an extraordinary journey of digestion which takes it along several yards of gut.

Your whole gut is an active muscular tube along which food can pass. It stretches from the back of your mouth to the anus. Many glands are attached to your gut and send their juices into it to help break down the food. Each section of this long passageway through the body has its own particular job to carry out, and its shape and the way it is organized depend on the job it does.

The food in your mouth is first chopped and ground up into small pieces by the chewing action of your tongue and teeth. Saliva flows from the salivary glands into your mouth and moistens chewed food so that it can be swallowed easily. It also contains a digestive enzyme (a kind of chemical juice) that starts to break down, or digest, the starches (complex carbohydrates) in your food.

When you swallow, a mouthful of food passes down your gullet (the esophagus). This is simply a connecting tube that takes food through the neck and chest regions to the abdomen, where the process of digestion starts in earnest. It takes food only a second or so to pass down the gullet to the stomach.

The food stays in the stomach for some time, being digested, before it is passed into the longest gut region—the small intestine. Tubes join the gut near the start of the small intestine; they bring secretions to it which are important for digestion. Bile, which is made by the liver, comes down the bile duct and digestive enzymes arrive from the pancreas. In the small intestine the breaking down of food continues and the useful parts, or nutrients, are absorbed into your body.

At the rear end of the small intestine the gut tube gets wider and is called the colon or large intestine. Here water is removed from the remains of the food so the undigested remnants become drier. The final indigestible wastes are formed into feces and stored at the end of the colon. When feces pass out of the anus, the food has completed its journey through the gut.

How long does food take to go through my body?

It takes most food a total of about 24 hours to pass right through your body. Some foods, especially liquids, move faster and others slightly more slowly. As they move through your body, the useful parts of food, the nutrients, are absorbed into your blood and carried around your body.

Some nutrients, for instance glucose and most vitamins, can be absorbed as they are. Many other nutrients—like proteins, fats and starches—are made up of bigger units, or molecules, and they cannot be absorbed in this form. That is why digestion has to take place. Digestion breaks down food molecules into smaller nutrients that can easily be absorbed by the lining of the gut.

Food comes in as a raw material and is ground up in the stomach, where it remains for about eight hours while serious digestion begins. It then passes to the small intestine, where two new sets of chemicals are added to the food. Bile, made in the liver and stored in the gall bladder, is mixed with digestive enzymes from the pancreas. The nutrients released by digestion go into the bloodstream and are moved to the liver for processing and storage. The food stays in the small intestine for about two hours.

The residue of food then passes to the colon, where it remains for the longest part of its digestive journey—about 14 hours in all. Water is absorbed from the food into the blood and the rest stored as waste, ready to leave via the anus.

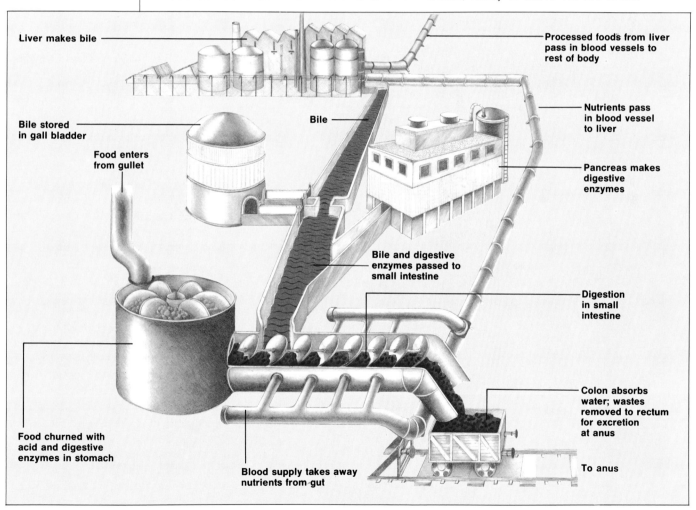

Liver makes bile

Bile stored in gall bladder

Food enters from gullet

Bile

Processed foods from liver pass in blood vessels to rest of body

Nutrients pass in blood vessel to liver

Pancreas makes digestive enzymes

Bile and digestive enzymes passed to small intestine

Digestion in small intestine

Colon absorbs water; wastes removed to rectum for excretion at anus

Food churned with acid and digestive enzymes in stomach

Blood supply takes away nutrients from gut

To anus

The industrial landscape of your gut is shown above. The processes that food undergoes are represented as parts of a factory complex for food processing. This emphasizes the linked jobs of the different parts of the gut, as well as those of the liver, gall bladder and pancreas. The breaking down of food makes digestion more of a destruction line than a production line, however!

Is it true that you can eat an apple while standing on your head?

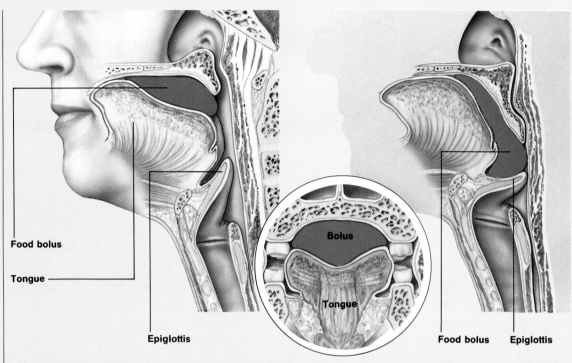

Food bolus

Tongue

Epiglottis

Bolus

Tongue

Food bolus   **Epiglottis**

Although it is *not* a very sensible thing to try—you could always choke—it is quite true that you can easily eat an apple and swallow it while you are standing on your head. You could even drink a glass of apple juice and swallow it while in the same upside-down position.

The fact is that it is not gravity that takes food through your gut. Instead, it is actually pushed along by muscles. This muscle-pushing system can just as easily move food upward (while you are standing on your head) as it can downward, while you are sitting or standing the right way up.

Swallowing is the first special part of the food-pushing action of the gut. It actually starts the food's journey down the gut tube and has to be carefully organized so that the food goes down the gullet and

Food bolus

Muscles in gut wall

Narrowing of gut wall muscles

Food bolus

This picture shows how food is pushed along the gut by the muscle action called peristalsis. The muscle layer in the wall of the gut has squeezed down to make a narrower constriction above the ball of food. This narrowing then moves downward, pushing food along in front of it.

How does food move through my gut?

Food is pushed through your gut by muscles. The whole of the gut tube, yard after yard of it, has layers of muscles in its wall. These muscles work automatically, controlled by a special part of the nervous system known as the autonomic system.

If there is food in the gut, it will be pushed along by these muscles, by a method called peristalsis. Just above a bolus of food in the gut, the muscles contract to make the gut narrower there. This constriction, or "waist," then moves downward along the gut. The wavelike movement, known as peristalsis, pushes the food along in front of it.

At any one time the gut will have many of these peristaltic contractions passing down it and moving food steadily along.

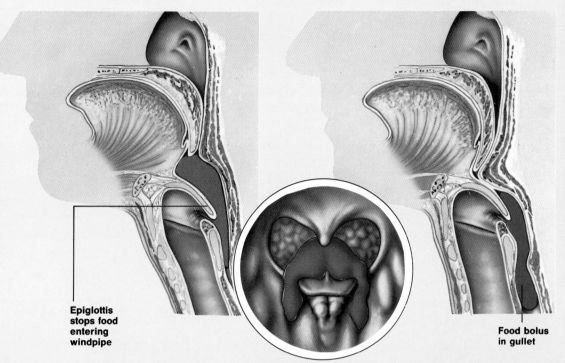

When you swallow, a ball of food (a bolus) at the back of the mouth is pushed backward by the tongue. At the same time the larynx (Adam's apple) rises, so that the flap called the epiglottis forms a lid over the top of the windpipe. With this protective cover in place, the bolus can safely pass down the gullet, and into the stomach.

Epiglottis stops food entering windpipe

Food bolus in gullet

not into your windpipe instead.

While you were growing as a minute embryo in your mother's womb, your lungs in fact started off as an outgrowth from the wall of the gut. These beginnings still show up now that you have grown: your windpipe and gullet still meet at the back of the throat and swallowing has to ensure that food does not "go down the wrong way"—that is, pass into the top of

the windpipe and make you choke.

Feel your throat as you swallow. You will find that your Adam's apple bobs up and then down again at the moment of swallowing. This is part of an automatic pattern of movements that shuts off the top of the windpipe as food passes. A flap of tissue called the epiglottis on top of the windpipe ensures that food passes down the gullet, not toward the lungs.

65

What is my stomach for?

Your stomach has several important jobs to perform—all of them to do with the handling of food. The stomach, which is located just below your diaphragm, is firstly a storage container for recently-eaten food. Food enters the stomach within seconds of being swallowed, but then it stays there for a considerable time.

While it is held in the stomach, several crucial things are done to the food. The stomach is very muscular and acts like a slow-churning food processor, stirring and squeezing the food until it turns it into a finely broken-up "slurry" or thick soup. To help in making this soup, the stomach wall produces several useful materials.

Mucus and fluid are mixed with the food to add to its liquid bulk. The wall also

secretes acid and a special digestive fluid. The acid—hydrochloric acid—sterilizes the food, killing almost all the germs you may have swallowed in or on your food. The acid also produces the right conditions inside the stomach for its digestive fluids to work. The acid-loving digestive chemical, or enzyme, in this fluid is called pepsin. Its purpose is to begin the breakdown of the proteins in your diet.

After an hour or more of churning, acid addition and protein digestion, the contents of the stomach—now called chyme—are passed for further processing to the small intestine. Small amounts of chyme are squeezed into the intestine through a muscular valve called the pyloric sphincter.

How do I digest my food?

You digest your food with the help of chemicals called digestive enzymes. Digestion is the breaking-down of large food units, or molecules, into smaller units that can be absorbed by your gut. The digestive enzymes are the special, active proteins (catalysts) made by your body to break up the large molecules.

Take, for example, the proteins in your diet. Egg white is mostly a protein called albumen. Each albumen molecule can be thought of as a necklace of beads, where each individual bead on the string is a useful nutrient molecule called an amino acid. Your gut cannot absorb an albumen molecule (the whole necklace) because it is too big. It can, though, absorb single amino acids—the individual beads of the necklace. Protein-splitting enzymes released into the gut can cut the necklace up into amino-acid beads which can then be absorbed.

The main protein-splitting enzymes are pepsin, made in the stomach, and another called trypsin, made by the pancreas. Starch-splitting enzymes which go to work on carbohydrates like those found in bread are present in saliva and in pancreatic secretions. Enzymes for cutting up fats such as those in butter are also produced by the pancreas.

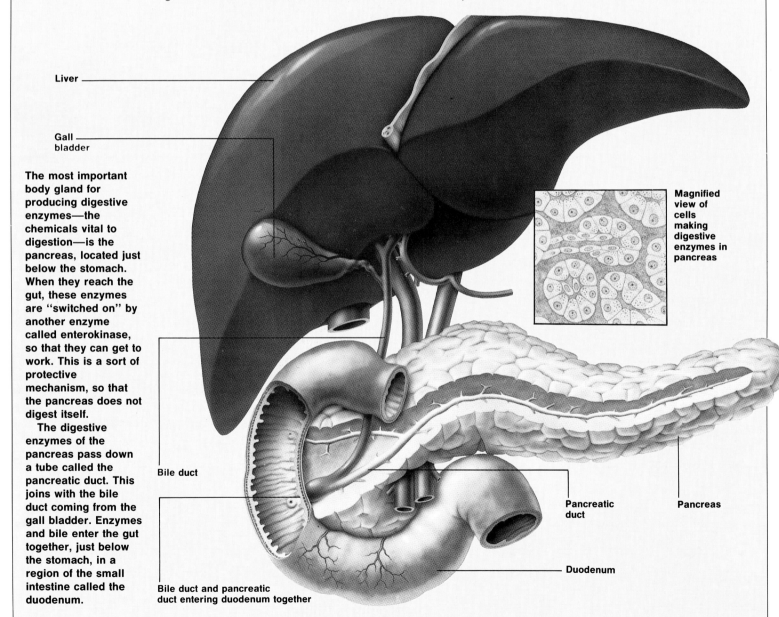

Liver

Gall bladder

The most important body gland for producing digestive enzymes—the chemicals vital to digestion—is the pancreas, located just below the stomach. When they reach the gut, these enzymes are "switched on" by another enzyme called enterokinase, so that they can get to work. This is a sort of protective mechanism, so that the pancreas does not digest itself.

The digestive enzymes of the pancreas pass down a tube called the pancreatic duct. This joins with the bile duct coming from the gall bladder. Enzymes and bile enter the gut together, just below the stomach, in a region of the small intestine called the duodenum.

Magnified view of cells making digestive enzymes in pancreas

Bile duct

Bile duct and pancreatic duct entering duodenum together

Pancreatic duct

Pancreas

Duodenum

67

Why does my stomach make noises when I'm hungry?

Your stomach and intestines are making noises all the time. They are made by the waves of muscle contractions that squeeze their way along the gut almost continuously.

As the squeezing actions move a mixture of food, liquids and gases along the gut, they make a quiet gurgling and sloshing noise, rather like those that any plumbing system makes as water passes through it. A doctor can hear this noise with a stethoscope.

The noises seem to get louder and much more obvious when you are hungry and have not eaten for a long time. You begin to hear the gurgles yourself—and people near you can often hear them too! The reason for this increase in volume is mainly the result of lack of food in the stomach. With no food there, the space inside the stomach contains a little fluid and much gas. Within a large, gas-filled space, the squeezing of peristalsis produces louder gurgles because the space acts as a vibrating sound-box.

68

Why do I get a stomach ache sometimes?

A stomach ache can be caused by a number of things, most quite trivial and only a few really serious. It is important to realize that a so-called "stomach ache," a dull or gripping pain in the abdomen, is only sometimes caused by problems in the stomach itself. In fact, troubles with any abdominal part of the gut can produce a "stomach ache."

Two common reasons for pain in this region are overactive muscle-squeezing (peristalsis), or inflammation of the gut. Several sorts of mild bacterial and viral infections of the gut can produce inflammation of the gut lining and therefore an increase in the strength of the contractions of peristalsis. If the inflammation spreads, the muscles in that part of the wall of your abdomen contract to try to hold the gut still. This contraction itself makes the pain worse as the abdomen gets tense.

Most "indigestion" seem to be caused by too much hydrochloric acid being made in the stomach. This can be caused by eating habits or by stress.

69

Why do some people have their appendix out?

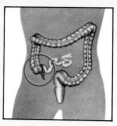

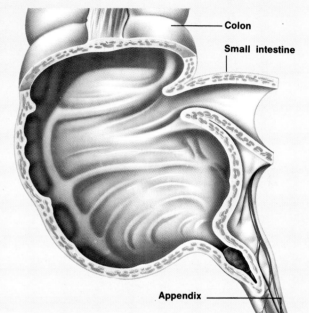

Colon

Small intestine

Appendix

Your appendix is a finger-shaped bulge of gut sticking out near the junction of the small and large intestines. It is 3–5 inches (8–12 cm) long, and hollow; it is larger in children than in adults.

No-one is quite sure what your appendix is there for, but some scientists think that it produces defensive white blood cells to attack germs in the gut. It is also possible that it was used long ago when humans ate more tough plant food, to help in the digestion of this material. Plant-eating animals like rabbits have a proportionally much larger appendix.

If the hollow center of the appendix gets blocked by undigested lumps of food, the organ itself gets inflamed. Germs trapped inside can then cause an infection. Both inflammation and infection give rise to acute pain in the appendix region.

Appendicitis is usually treated by a simple operation in which the appendix is cut out. It is done as swiftly as possible in case the inflamed appendix bursts, in which case there would be a risk of a serious infection of the abdomen.

How big is my gut?

Because the body needs a huge surface area to absorb all the nutrients from food, the inner lining of the small intestine is like a tennis court folded inside a tube! The total absorbing surface of the small intestine in fact measures 200 times more than the entire skin surface of your body.

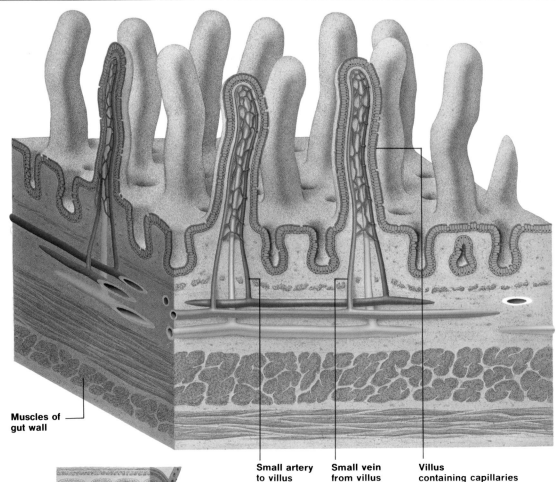

Muscles of gut wall

Small artery to villus

Small vein from villus

Villus containing capillaries

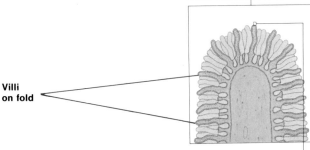

Folds in gut wall

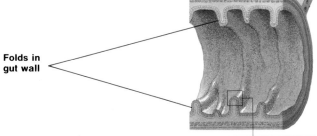

Villi on fold

Microvilli on gut cell surface

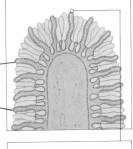

The total length of the gut is around 30 feet (9 meters). The longest section of it is the "small" intestine which is usually estimated at about 25 feet (7.5 meters). The colon, or "large" intestine, is about 5 feet (1.5 meters), and thus much shorter than the small intestine, but it is three times as wide, measuring 2½ inches (7 cm) in diameter. It seems likely, though, that the living, moving gut is shorter than these figures suggest because when the gut's muscles are contracting, the gut gets shorter.

The small intestine is, however, extensive in a more subtle and interesting way than just length. It has a gigantic internal surface area. The total area of its inner lining is about 300 square yards (250 square meters)—larger than a doubles tennis court!

This enormous area is needed to absorb useful nutrients all over the inner surface of the small intestine. But how is it all packed into your abdomen? The answer is with folds upon folds upon folds. The inner lining of the intestine is folded into its hollow center, with shelf-like ridges that greatly increase its internal area. The whole of the gut lining is, in turn, thrown into minute finger-shaped bulges called villi, which further increase the total area. Finally, the cells covering the villi are themselves covered with extensions called microvilli—yet another magnification of the whole surface area.

What is the liver for?

REAR VIEW OF WHOLE LIVER

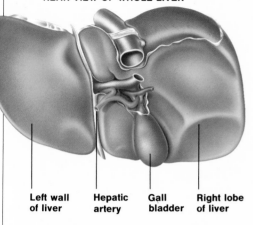

Left wall of liver

Hepatic artery

Gall bladder

Right lobe of liver

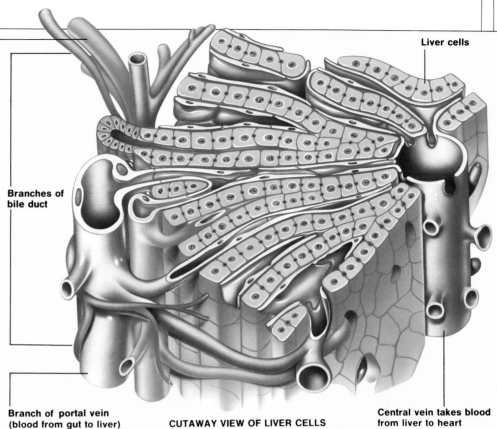

Hepatic artery (blood from heart to liver)

Liver cells

Branches of bile duct

Branch of portal vein (blood from gut to liver)

CUTAWAY VIEW OF LIVER CELLS

Central vein takes blood from liver to heart

The liver carries out a huge number of different jobs in the body. Some have to do with blood, others have to do with food, and yet others have to do with protecting your body against poisonous substances. Basically, if the body needs one substance to be turned into another, the liver is a sort of general chemical factory which is able to carry out the job.

Your liver is a large, reddish-purple organ tucked under your diaphragm and going over and around your stomach. It is in fact the largest organ in your body, weighing between three and four pounds (1.3–1.8 kilograms) in an adult. It has a large blood supply and acts to remove, or make harmless, unwanted or dangerous substances in the blood. The liver is the main

place where the poisons that have been taken into the body get broken down or neutralized.

As well as destroying things, the liver is a great manufacturing center, too. One of its major products is the liquid secretion called bile, which gets transported to the bag called the gall bladder on the liver's surface for storage. Bile is finally passed down the bile duct to the small intestine to help with digestion.

Bile works like a natural detergent, helping fats and oils in food to be "emulsified" or broken down into tiny droplets and mixed, with water, into a fine soup. This then allows fat-splitting enzymes to work on the "soup" and to break it down into substances called fatty acids and glycerol which can be absorbed in the bloodstream.

How do the nutrients in my food get from my gut to the rest of my body?

The useful nutrients are needed for the building up, growth and repair of our bodies and to give us energy. They are produced from our food with the aid of digestive enzymes in the gut and are then absorbed into the blood across the gigantic surface area of the small intestine. The nutrients pass from the gut into the gut's tiny blood vessels.

Most of these blood vessels then join together and lead to the liver. This unique piece of blood supply going from the gut

to the liver—the only blood vessels in the body which do not start or finish at the heart—is called the hepatic portal system. Thus the nutrients absorbed from the gut go first to the liver.

The liver acts as a chemical processing plant for these nutrients. Some are passed onto the rest of the blood system, and therefore the rest of the body, unchanged. Others are transformed into new useful materials before being passed on and yet others are stored as a food reserve.

Do I need vitamin pills to stay healthy?

No, not if you eat wholesome and varied meals. Any ordinary diet containing fresh and nourishing food provides plenty of the vitamins and minerals you need to grow and stay healthy.

Vitamins are vital nutrients that you need only in small quantities, measured in milligrams or micrograms (thousandths or millionths of a gram), per day. They are crucial for health and growth because your body cannot make them out of other substances. They are used in the body for a range of essential jobs, such as building strong bones and teeth, and for helping important body chemicals to work.

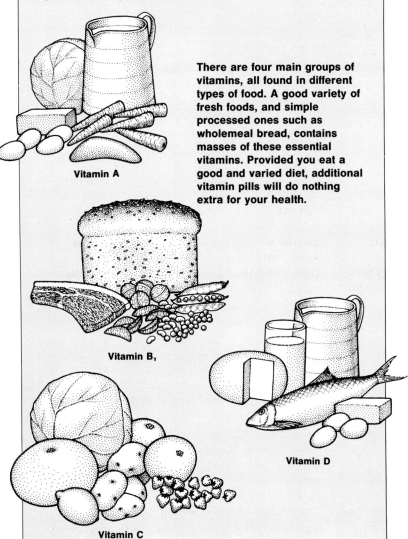

There are four main groups of vitamins, all found in different types of food. A good variety of fresh foods, and simple processed ones such as wholemeal bread, contains masses of these essential vitamins. Provided you eat a good and varied diet, additional vitamin pills will do nothing extra for your health.

Vitamin A

Vitamin B₁

Vitamin D

Vitamin C

Why do we have to eat so many different kinds of food?

We eat a great variety of foods because our bodies need a wide range of different nutrients. Only by eating a mixture of different types of food can we be sure of getting all these necessary materials.

As well as the thirteen or so important vitamins required in minute quantities, your body needs a number of nutrients in far greater amounts.

It needs energy-providing foods, which are normally a mixture of starches (digested into sugars) and fats or oils. Protein-containing foods, such as meat, fish or eggs, are needed for growth, and for the repair of body organs.

We also need fiber or rough foods, such as wholemeal bread and brown rice, which aid the workings of the gut or digestive system. Finally, we need a large quantity of water and a wide range of minerals including calcium, phosphorus, potassium, iron and iodine. These are essential for healthy teeth, bones, and blood.

How long can someone live without food?

Many weeks—or even months—depending on exactly what is meant by living without food.

If someone completely stopped eating and drinking, they would die in a few days because they would lose too much water and too many minerals from their body. These would be lost mainly through the production of urine but also through evaporation of sweat from the skin surface. If the body's fluids are not replaced, this quickly threatens a person's life.

Provided water was available, a person could survive for much longer because the fluid level in his or her body could be kept up. Without food, the body would start to slowly use up its food stores.

The first stores to be used would be fat from under the skin and the special starch glycogen, from the liver, and the person would gradually become thinner. The body would then start breaking down muscle and more crucial organs to keep going. But once these internal reserves were exhausted, the already-wasted person would die.

Why are some of my friends fatter than me although they don't eat as much?

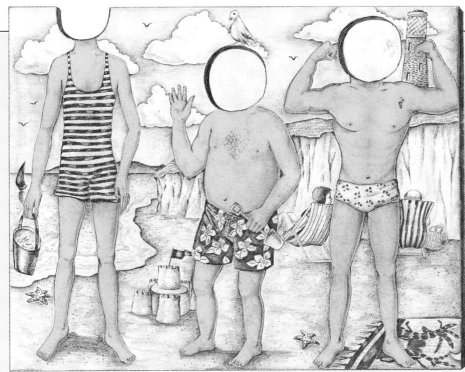

DIFFERENT PHYSIQUES

If we compare people of roughly the same height, there are several reasons for variations in size. Firstly, there is your general "build," which has to do with the size of your bones and muscles. To a certain extent, you inherit your basic build from your parents and the three extreme "types" are illustrated above. These are exaggerated, but we all tend to one type or another. Ectomorphs (left) are usually tall and thin with a narrow body and thin limbs; they tend not to store body fat. Endomorphs (center) are stocky and rounded, with short limbs; they tend to accumulate fat. Mesomorphs (right) are strongly built and muscular, with little fat.

Broadly-built people with large, well-developed muscles look big for their height because of the muscle bulk in their arms, legs, and torso. However, whether your muscles are well-developed, or allowed to become feeble, depends to a great extent on how much you exercise.

Although there is some genetic (that is, inherited) background to how fat you are, fatness has much more to do with the amount and type of food you eat. Fat people who appear to eat less than you have perhaps inherited an endomorph build from their parents, but they may be consuming large amounts of energy-rich foods, such as fats, starches and alcohol.

What happens to the undigested parts of my food?

They are changed into feces (stools) and gotten rid of, or excreted, through the anus. Feces and defecation are rather taboo subjects and are often treated as a subject for embarrassment or jokes. But feces are simply the end-point of the whole marvelous business of getting the useful parts of food into your body.

All factories have waste-products and the food-processing factory of your gut is no exception. Much of the vegetable fiber in your diet is undigestible. Along with other parts of your food that cannot be broken down, the fiber is compressed into a paste-like form in the colon or large intestine. Most of the water in the paste is reabsorbed by the colon and you are left with the dry residue—feces.

Feces are stored in the end part of the colon, called the rectum. Once or twice a day you feel the need to defecate, when the amount in your rectum builds up. You defecate by loosening the valve muscle (sphincter) at the opening, the anus, and squeezing out the feces by pushing down with your abdominal muscles.

Where in the body is urine made?

Kidney

Ureter

Bladder

Urethra

Urine, the main liquid waste of the body, is made in the kidneys. You have a pair of kidneys and they lie at the back of your abdomen, on either side of your backbone, well protected by your ribs.

Each kidney is about 4 inches (10 cm) long and weighs about 5 ounces (140 g). They are "kidney-shaped," in other words the shape of a string-bean seed, with one convex side and a depression in the opposite side.

Every day an adult's kidneys produce about 3 pints (1.5 liters) of urine, and this passes down a thin tube called a ureter—there is one leading from each kidney. The two ureters separately join the bladder, where urine is stored before it is passed out of the body.

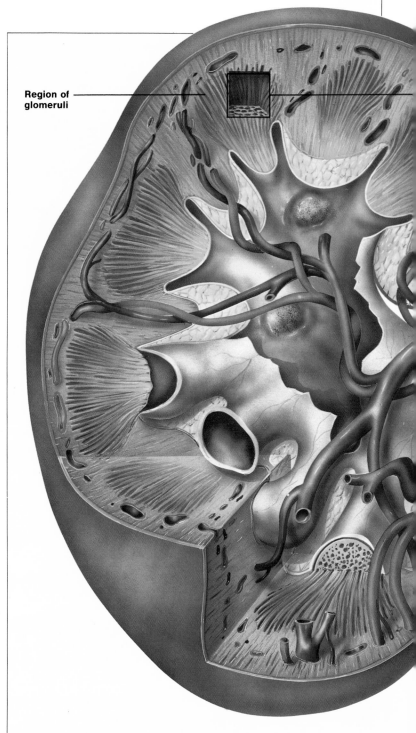

Region of glomeruli

The internal structure of a kidney, revealed in this cross-section, shows its large blood supply.

A massive artery, known as the renal artery, brings blood in large quantities to the kidney. An equally large renal vein takes it back to the heart, but only after it has been filtered to make urine. The urine is collected into a series of large tubes or ducts, which join up to form the ureter leading to the bladder.

All of the outer layer of the kidney consists of more than a million tiny filtering units called glomeruli. In these, water and wastes are filtered out of blood to start the production of urine.

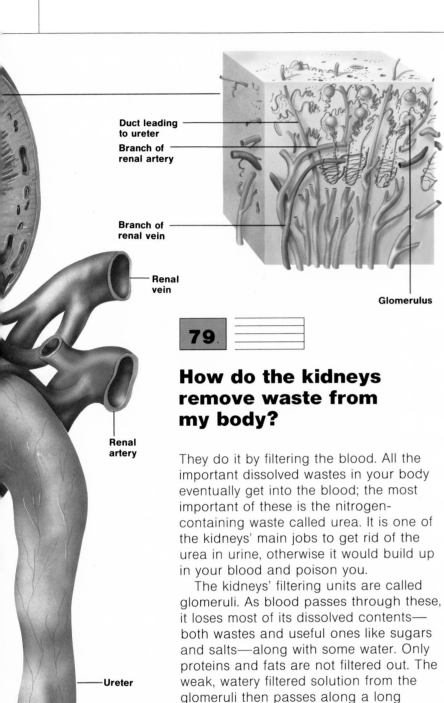

Duct leading
to ureter

Branch of
renal artery

Branch of
renal vein

Renal
vein

Glomerulus

Renal
artery

Ureter

Why do girls and boys have different places for urine to come out?

Because these openings do other jobs too: the organs in this area are also sex organs used for making babies. The upper parts of the urine-making organs of girls and boys are exactly the same, in fact. Both have two kidneys, two ureters and a bladder. In both, a single tube, the urethra, leads from the bottom of the bladder to remove urine.

It is the outlet of the urethra which seems very different. In girls, the opening is tucked away, normally unseen, near the top of the opening of the vagina. In boys, it is far more obvious, as a hole at the end of the penis. The penis is the passageway for sperm as well as urine and it needs to be the shape it is so that it can take sperm into the mother's vagina.

A woman's vagina is both the way in for the sperm, and the way out for a baby which has developed in the womb, when it is time for it to be born. The urine outlet of the urethra is in fact kept separate from this important passageway.

79.

How do the kidneys remove waste from my body?

They do it by filtering the blood. All the important dissolved wastes in your body eventually get into the blood; the most important of these is the nitrogen-containing waste called urea. It is one of the kidneys' main jobs to get rid of the urea in urine, otherwise it would build up in your blood and poison you.

The kidneys' filtering units are called glomeruli. As blood passes through these, it loses most of its dissolved contents—both wastes and useful ones like sugars and salts—along with some water. Only proteins and fats are not filtered out. The weak, watery filtered solution from the glomeruli then passes along a long looping tube (a tubule). As it does so, it gives back to the surrounding blood vessels all the useful substances.

The urea, though, remains. By the time it reaches the ends of the tubules, the filtered solution has been converted into urea-rich urine to be passed to the ureter—and then to the bladder. Of the daily 350 pints (200 liters) of fluid made by the filtering action of the glomeruli, only 3 pints (1.5 liters) ends up as urine.

81

How much water is there in my body?

There is more water than anything else in your body—it is a surprising thought that you are mostly made of water! The actual amount depends on your body size, but the body of an average-sized adult contains about 76 pints (43 liters) of water—or 60 percent of their weight.

You might think that blood holds most of the water in the body but, in fact, the blood's plasma (the fluid part in which the red and white blood cells float around) contains only around 6 pints (3.5 liters) of water. The greatest quantity of water is actually inside the body's cells; this liquid is known as the intracellular fluid, and it accounts for some 51 pints (29 liters) in the tiny spaces between all cells, and is called the interstitial fluid.

You can only "top up" your body's water through your mouth. You drink water straight, or in other drinks, or you take it in as part of solid foods. (A food such as lettuce is 90 percent water.) But you also lose water constantly, in one of three ways. About a pint (half a liter) is breathed out as water vapor from your moist lungs, 3 pints (1.5 liters) leave your body as urine, and another pint (half a liter) evaporates from your skin surface.

82

Why do stools smell?

The smell of stools partly reflects the food you have eaten, but it is mainly created by the billions of microscopic organisms called bacteria in your gut.

Stools or feces are the final waste product of the gut. They consist of the undigestible part of the food you take in, but their other main component is bacteria. There are huge numbers of bacteria in the gut, particularly in the colon; most of them are harmless or even useful in helping with digestion or producing B vitamins.

Your feces stay in the rectum, at the end of your colon, for some considerable time. While they are there, the bacteria in them can partially digest substances in your feces, and in doing so, they make smelly odors as their waste products.

The bacteria also produce a gas as they break down the food residue. This escapes, at intervals, as wind via the anus.

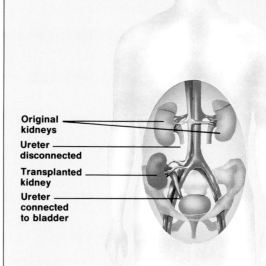

Original kidneys
Ureter disconnected
Transplanted kidney
Ureter connected to bladder

83

What is a kidney transplant?

In a kidney transplant operation, a new, healthy kidney is placed in the body of a person whose own kidneys are damaged.

When kidneys are damaged by disease, they are unable to remove wastes from the blood properly. This can be a very dangerous situation. If urea levels build up in the blood because of damaged, inactive kidneys, this waste can poison the body and could cause death. Some kidney diseases can be effectively treated with medicines. But others cannot, and one alternative is a kidney transplant.

In this operation, the diseased kidneys are usually left in place and a new kidney and its attached urine-draining tube or ureter are placed in the pelvis. The kidney is joined up to the large artery and vein that serve the leg, while the new ureter is joined to the bladder. The replacement kidney can come from a close relative (who can remain healthy with only one kidney), or from a person who has just died. The person who gives the kidney is known as a "donor."

In a normal kidney transplant operation, kidneys are not "swapped." The old ones are left in place. The transplanted kidney from a donor is surgically placed in the pelvis. It has to be connected to blood vessels and to the bladder.

Donor and patient must have genes as similar to one another as possible to prevent the body rejecting the new kidney. Rejection can also be stopped by special anti-rejection drugs.

How does a kidney machine work?

A kidney machine takes blood from a patient's circulation, filters out wastes like urea from it, and then passes the cleaned-up blood back into a vein. In the cleaning process—called dialysis—the blood passes across a membrane, which lets urea pass through and keeps the useful parts of the blood behind.

It works more or less like the living kidneys do. The dialysis machine, as it is called, removes waste materials such as urea from the blood, but leaves behind the useful materials like sugars, cells and proteins. This complex piece of apparatus keeps sufferers from severe kidney disease alive when their kidneys stop working. It takes over the waste removal job of the damaged organs by a filtering technique called "dialysis."

The treatment makes huge demands on a patient's time and courage because he or she has to be connected to the machine for some 16 hours at a time, and for about three sessions every week. Dialysis on a kidney machine is often used to keep a patient healthy until a good kidney can be found for a transplant operation.

In dialysis, the wastes are separated from the blood. The machine consists of tubing and pumps which enable the patient's blood to be pushed past a large area of membrane, on the other side of which is a special salt and sugar solution. Wastes such as urea pass through the membrane, but useful components are kept back.

Joining the machine to the patient's blood supply is in itself a difficult problem. Often the surgeon joins an artery and vein in the skin to each other, which makes connections to this section of blood vessels easier and less dangerous. Drugs are also added to the blood to stop it clotting in the machine.

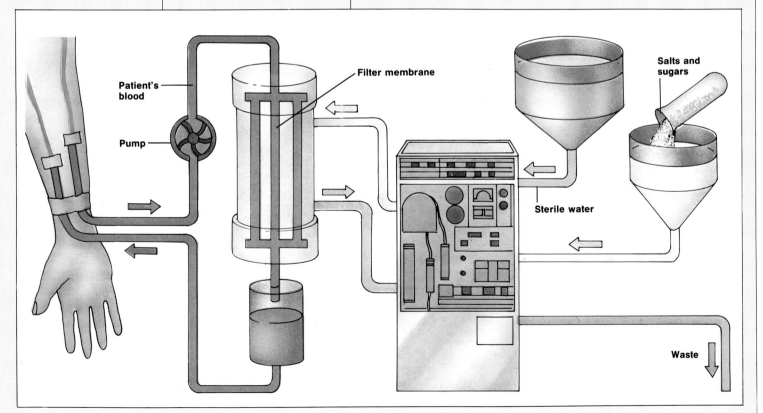

Patient's blood

Pump

Filter membrane

Salts and sugars

Sterile water

Waste

85

Are there only five senses?

No, you actually have more than five different senses, but there are five main ones. These are: seeing (vision), hearing, taste, smell, and the sense of touch. With these senses you find out a great deal about the world around you. The extra senses include the sense of pain, balance, position and temperature.

Of the five main senses, four depend

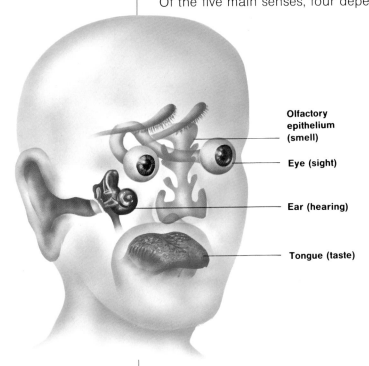

Olfactory epithelium (smell)

Eye (sight)

Ear (hearing)

Tongue (taste)

The four sense organs are located in your head. Each organ is specialized for a particular task: the eyes take in information for seeing, the ears for hearing, the tongue for tasting and the nose for smelling.

on special organs, called sense organs, found in the head. Touch is spread all over the outside of your body. But you do not have the same sensitivity all over: the fingertips are the most sensitive part, since they have the most nerve endings in them. The fingers, toes and lips are also very sensitive.

All sense organs work by sending information about their own interpretation of the world back to the brain. The information is picked up by the nerve endings and flows back to the brain as signals in the so-called sensory nerves. Only when the brain gets this information and processes it does the sense operate, and you "feel" or become aware of something. In other words, the eye does not "see" on its own: you see only when your eyes and brain are working together.

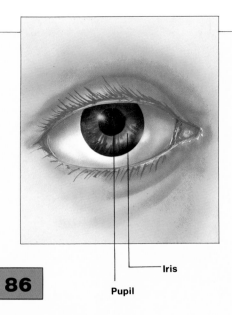

Iris

86

Pupil

Why are eyes different colors?

The colored part of your eye, the ring between the black pupil in the center and the white of the eye, is called the iris. Iris was the Greek goddess of the rainbow, so the name is a good one because the iris can be many different shades: it can be blue, brown or almost black, or sometimes a flecked mixture of these colors, such as "hazel." There are other variations, with blue eyes sometimes showing as gray or green and brown eyes as amber.

Despite this range of appearances, a single colored substance called melanin produces them all. Melanin itself comes in tiny dark brown granules in the cells of the iris. If there are many of them the iris looks dark brown or black. Smaller quantities produce a light brown color.

So how can brown granules make blue eyes? They are blue for the same reason that the sky or the sea looks blue. When light passes through something transparent with tiny particles in it, the particles only scatter the blues and greens in the light. So just as tiny particles in the water make the ocean look blue, and dust in the air makes the sky blue, a few granules of melanin in the iris make an iris blue. So blue eyes are those with little melanin, too little for its own color to show up.

87

How do my eyes work?

You can see with your eyes because they capture images of the outside world in much the same way that a camera does. The eye is a darkened hollow sphere with a round hole at the front—the pupil—into which light can pass. Just inside this hole is a lens, working like a camera lens.

The lens in a camera throws an image of the outside scene onto photographic film. In the eye, the lens throws an image onto the back of the eyeball, covered by a layer of cells called the retina. These cells are sensitive to light—its brightness and color. When an image hits them, they code the image into a nerve signal which, in a fraction of a second, is sent to the brain along the optic nerve. The brain then uses these signals to enable us to see.

The picture on the retina is always upside down, because of the way the lens works. But your brain automatically turns it the right way up before you "see" it.

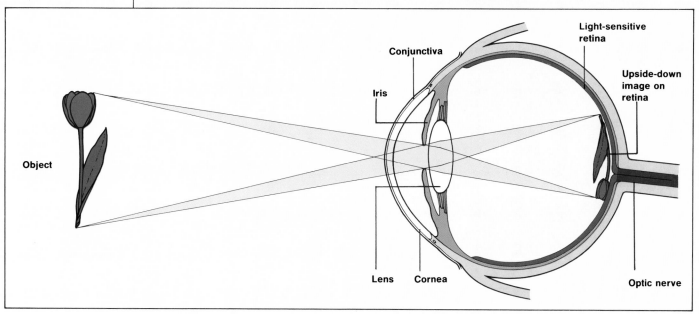

Conjunctiva
Iris
Light-sensitive retina
Upside-down image on retina
Object
Lens
Cornea
Optic nerve

88

How do they move so quickly?

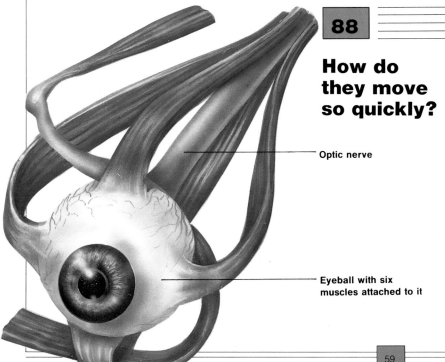

Optic nerve

Eyeball with six muscles attached to it

To see something as clearly as possible, the eyes must be pointing straight at it. If you want to study something closely, you can move your head so that your eyes line up with it. But fine movements of the eyes can go on even when the head is still.

Look at someone else's eyes when he or she is reading or playing a video game. They are constantly on the move, flickering rapidly to point first in one direction and then another. These movements are made possible by the six muscles that hold each eyeball in position in its socket in the skull.

If you look at an eye from the front and imagine it was a globe, there are north, south, east and west pulling muscles. There are also two which pull the eye crosswise. Several muscles usually work together and they can instantly point the eyes in any direction.

Why are tears salty?

Tears come from glands called tear glands, which lie hidden under the upper eyelids. The liquid they make washes over the eyes to keep them moist and free from dirt and infection; being salty helps its antiseptic properties. Tears are released all the time, day and night, whether we are happy or sad.

In keeping the front, exposed surface of the eye continually wet, tears stop the delicate, transparent skin over the front of the eye—the conjunctiva—from drying out and being damaged or infected. This washing with tears means that the front of the eye is also well lubricated, which ensures that the eyelids can slip smoothly and quickly over the eye without causing any roughness or scratching.

To keep the eyeball moist, and to keep it clean by washing away dust and other particles, the tears flow in a thin film down over the eye surface. The film is spread evenly over the eyeball as you blink, which happens automatically every few seconds. The tears then drain away down into two tiny openings at the inner edge of the eye, next to the bridge of the nose.

These holes are the entrances to the tear ducts, which are like drainage channels down which old, dirty tears are flushed away. The tear ducts carry them into the nose, from where they are constantly swallowed, or blown out, along with other nose secretions.

What makes the black part of my eye get bigger and smaller?

Iris open

Iris closed

The two sets of diagrams show, on the left, a vertical section through the eye, and, on the right, the eye seen from the front.

For the wide pupil (top) to close down, the iris extends inward to cut out more of the light entering the eye (bottom). This automatic control of "exposure" means that the eyes can see well in both bright and relatively dim light.

The dark circle in the middle of your eyes is called the pupil. It is where the light actually gets into your eye, enabling you to see. The colored ring of tissue—the iris—surrounding the pupil is what makes the pupil change size.

The pupil itself is just a hole, so it cannot change shape by itself. What alters is the outer edge of the hole formed by the iris. The iris acts like a kind of shutter, which opens and closes to let more or less light into the round hole, depending on the brightness outside.

The iris is made up of muscles which both circle the pupil and radiate out from it. In bright light, the circular muscles contract and the hole squeezes to a smaller shape to let in just enough light to see but not enough to damage the delicate retina. In dim light, the radiating muscles contract, making the iris smaller, and the pupil widens to let in as much light as possible.

These changes happen without your thinking about it. Sit a friend in a dimly lit room for a few minutes: his or her pupils will expand to a large size. Now switch on the light and watch them immediately become smaller. The iris is operating automatically, like the exposure control on a camera, to ensure that the correct amount of light enters the eye.

This front view of the eye (left) shows the tear gland, which makes tears, and the tear ducts which carry them away. The view (right) shows the eyelid and the protective eyelashes which, when touched, cause the eyelids to blink shut.

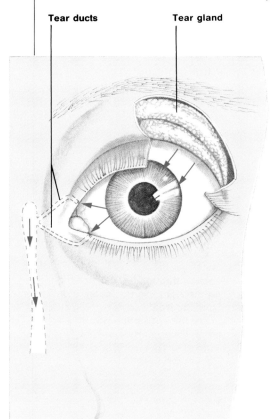

Tear ducts   Tear gland

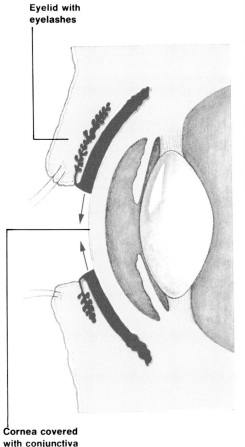

Eyelid with eyelashes

Cornea covered with conjunctiva

91

Why can't I stop blinking however hard I try?

You cannot stop yourself blinking because the blinking reflex is so crucial that it cannot be over-ridden. Like a factory's automatic safety system, such as sprinklers in a paint factory, it cannot be turned to manual because the sprinklers are so important. The eyes are our most vital sense, and blinking is their instinctive protective device. It has to happen all the time in order to spread a fresh film of tear fluid over the eyeball. The tears wash dust and germs from the eye and keep the conjunctiva constantly moist.

As well as the continual blinking, the eyelashes provide a sensitive first screen of defenses for the front of the eye. If anything touches them, you blink, and the blink shuts down the protective curtains of the eyelids over the eye. You also blink instinctively if you see something fast moving toward you. Even a loud noise could mean that something dangerous is flying toward the eyes, so a blink is the brain's "better safe than sorry" reflex.

92

Why do I cry when I'm sad?

We do not really know. Normally, the tear glands make tears at exactly the same rate as they flow away down the tear ducts. This means that the eyes stay moist but do not overflow with the watery secretion.

When you are sad or in pain, you flood your eyes with tears, just as you do if you get some grit in your eyes or if you stand over chopped onions and your eyes "water." You make more tears than your tear ducts to the nose can cope with, the tears overflow, and you cry.

With the grit, there is an obvious reason for the extra tears: they help to flush the grit out. They also contain a natural germ-killer, and so help to stop infection.

There is no such logical explanation, though, for crying when you are upset or sad. While all animals that live in air produce tears to keep their eyes moist, only humans produce emotional tears through crying. Perhaps crying is a signal by which you can show other people how unhappy—or happy— you are.

How do I hear?

Your ears are designed to pick up and detect sounds, but the sound waves first have to go on a strange journey through the tunnels of your ear. They then have to travel inside your head to the brain to be analyzed before you can truly hear anything.

The part of your ear that you can see – the outer ear flap called the pinna – is only one small part of the mechanism of your hearing system. It acts like an antenna, picking up and concentrating sound waves in the air. It funnels them down your ear canal – the "hole" in your ear.

At the end of the canal is your eardrum. This membrane is aptly named, since it is stretched across the canal like a taut drum skin. As sound waves hit it, the drum vibrates.

Joined to the inside of the eardrum is a chain of three tiny bones – the smallest in the body. They vibrate in sympathy with the eardrum but they also enlarge or amplify the vibrations. The last of the three bones – the stirrup – is connected to another stretched membrane, the oval window, whose vibrations send liquid in a coiled tube deep in the bones of the skull.

This coil, which looks like a snail shell, is called the cochlea. It is the region of the ear that actually "hears." It is this part that changes vibrations into nerve messages about sound that go to the brain, to be sorted and made sense of. Different wave patterns are formed with sounds of different loudness and pitch, so the brain can "hear" these differences.

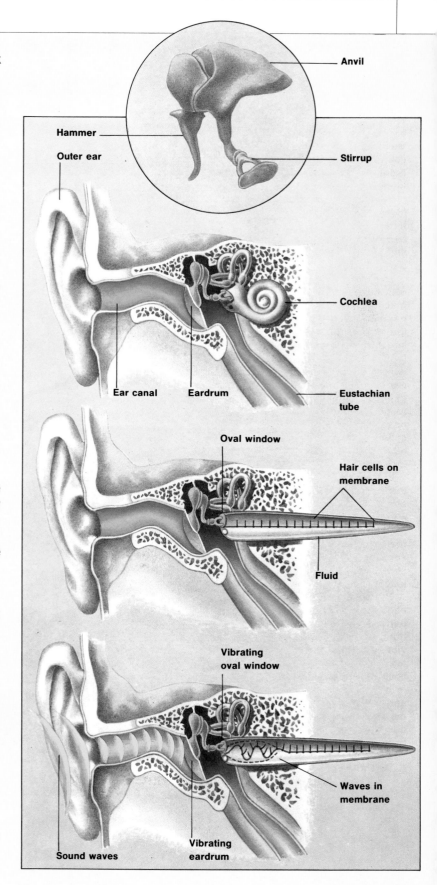

Anvil

Hammer

Outer ear

Stirrup

Cochlea

Ear canal

Eardrum

Eustachian tube

Oval window

Hair cells on membrane

Fluid

Vibrating oval window

Waves in membrane

Sound waves

Vibrating eardrum

The pictures on the left explain how the workings of the ear let you hear – whether it is a pin dropping or the loudest rock group.

The top inset shows, highly magnified, the three tiny bones that carry and amplify vibrations in the middle part of the ear.

The top cutaway picture shows the three main sections of the ear. The outer ear is the ear flap you can see and the ear canal. It finishes at the eardrum. The middle ear contains the chain of bones, and is linked to the air spaces of the nose via a tunnel called the Eustachian tube. The inner ear includes the cochlea.

In the middle picture the cochlea has been straightened out to show what is inside it. It contains a sheet, or membrane, with sensitive hairs stretched along its length.

The bottom picture shows that when the ear picks up sounds, the oval window vibrates. This jiggles the liquid in the cochlea, and the sheet or membrane waves up and down, triggering the hairs, which send nerve messages to the brain.

94

Why do I feel dizzy after spinning around?

The innermost part of the ear not only contains the cochlea, which hears sounds, it also possesses delicate curved tubes – all filled with liquid – called the semi-circular canals. These, and other nearby tubes, give you a sense of balance and of movement, even when your eyes are shut. When you move your head, liquid is sent down the canals. This stimulates the sense hairs, which send signals to the brain.

If you spin round then stop suddenly, you feel dizzy because the liquid inside the semi-circular canals carries on moving for a while after you stop. This movement of liquid falsely signals to the brain that you are still spinning. You know that you are not, so you feel this confusion as dizziness.

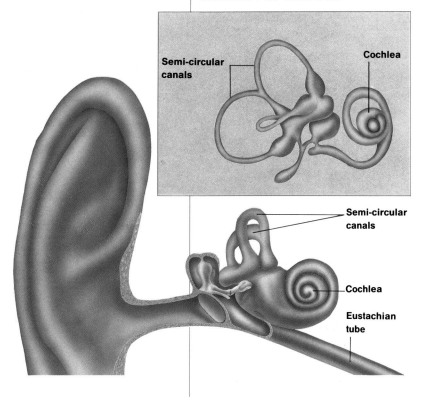

Semi-circular canals

Cochlea

The fluid-filled semi-circular canals are connected to the tubing of the sound-sensing cochlea. In each region nerve messages are created, and sent to the brain, when the sense hairs are stimulated – either by sound or by movement.

Semi-circular canals

Cochlea

Eustachian tube

95

Why do my ears pop when I go up in an aircraft?

Your ears may pop when you fly because of what happens to your eardrums. There is air on both sides of the eardrum since the inner side of it is connected to the inner spaces of your nose by the Eustachian tube. Normally, air pressure is the same on both sides of the eardrum.

When an aircraft takes off, the air pressure drops slightly in the cabin. This means that there is now a higher pressure in the air inside the eardrum than in that outside it, and the eardrum bulges. But the body has a failsafe mechanism to help to cope with this problem. As you swallow, the Eustachian tube widens, lowering the pressure of the air inside it, and the eardrum "pops" back into its correct place.

96

Is it true that loud disco music can damage your hearing?

Yes. If you are close to very loud, amplified sounds of any sort for a long time, you can become partially deafened. Several famous rock stars have admitted that their careers have damaged their own hearing.

Your ears have some defenses against loud sound which attempt to stop damage to the delicate, vibration-sensitive hair cells deep inside them. In particular, there are small muscles in the middle ear which can "turn down" the volume of sounds. They can do this by altering the movements of the tiny bones in this part of the ear. When a loud sound strikes, these muscles prevent the bones from vibrating. This means that the force of the soundwaves is lessened by the time it gets to the cochlea where the sensitive hairs are.

Constant loud sounds, though, can break through this defensive barrier and damage the hairs in the cochlea. They simply get shaken too hard.

To some extent this damage is short-term. After a very loud rock concert, your ears will be considerably less sensitive for a matter of hours or days, but will then return to normal. But if you are continually at loud concerts and discos—or working with a pneumatic drill without ear plugs—some of the damage never heals.

NOISE LEVELS

Decibels

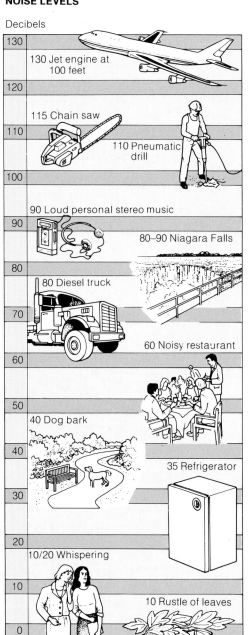

130	130 Jet engine at 100 feet
120	
110	115 Chain saw / 110 Pneumatic drill
100	
90	90 Loud personal stereo music
80	80–90 Niagara Falls / 80 Diesel truck
70	
60	60 Noisy restaurant
50	
40	40 Dog bark / 35 Refrigerator
30	
20	
10	10/20 Whispering / 10 Rustle of leaves
0	

Sound is measured in decibels. This is a complex measure in which every increase of three decibels means a doubling of loudness.

Human ears are sensitive to an incredibly wide range of volumes, the loudest being some ten billion times louder than the softest sounds we can hear. It is only the very loudest sounds, ones over 120 decibels, that are really dangerous to hearing. Close to a speaker at a disco or rock concert, you could be exposed to exactly that level.

97

Which part of my nose detects smells?

The part of your nose that can detect smells and odors is one that you cannot see. It consists of two patches of sense cells, called the olfactory epithelium, right at the top of the spaces inside your nose. Each patch is only about the size of a small postage stamp. Its sense cells send nerve messages into the brain. These smelling zones are located roughly beneath the bridge of the nose.

Most of the outer part of the nose and its complicated inner airspaces have nothing to do with your sense of smell. They are really just an "air conditioning plant" to warm, clean and moisten air before it goes into your lungs.

The cutaway picture of the nose shows the complicated airspaces inside it. Right at the top of those spaces are the two patches of olfactory epithelium with which you detect smells.

Olfactory nerves from brain   Olfactory epithelium   Airspace of nose

How does it do this?

The olfactory epithelium can detect scents because it is made of special sense cells which can respond to smelly substances. Everybody has about ten million of these sense cells, which are actually an outgrowth of the brain. They are the only part of the brain which ever comes into direct contact with the outside world.

Each sense cell sticks out into the air space of the nose, protected only by a thin film of the watery substance, mucus, made in the nose. Projecting into the mucus are thin tufts called cilia. These are the parts of the sense cells that are actually stimulated by the smelly molecules.

When you smell a rose, odor molecules from the rose dissolve in the mucus covering the epithelium. From here they contact the cilia of the sense cells and make them send nerve messages to the brain. You then experience the scent of the rose.

The tangled mass of hairlike cilia on the sense cells in your nose actually pick up smells. They are covered by a thin, protective layer of mucus.

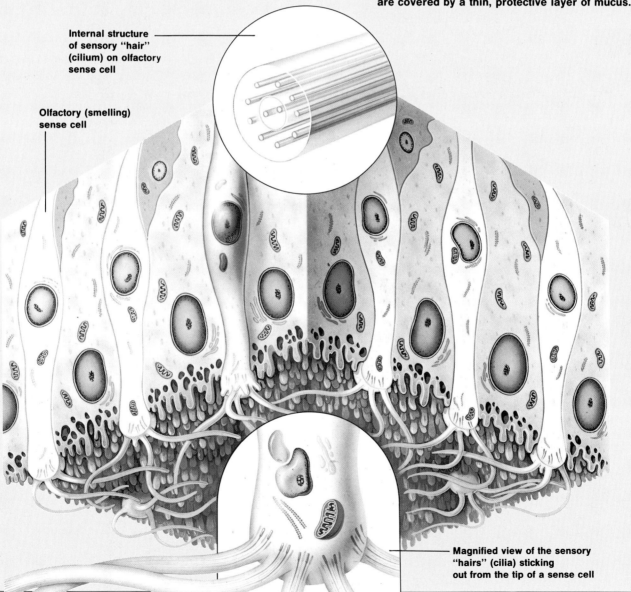

Internal structure of sensory "hair" (cilium) on olfactory sense cell

Olfactory (smelling) sense cell

Magnified view of the sensory "hairs" (cilia) sticking out from the tip of a sense cell

99

Why do I need to sniff to smell a rose rather than breathing normally?

"Sniff" for smelling

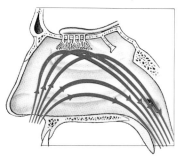

1. During a sniff, air and odors are drawn to the top of the nose spaces where the olfactory epithelium is located.

Shallow breathing

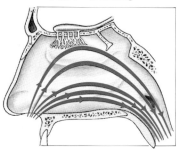

2. During shallow breathing, most air and odors bypass the top of the nose spaces.

Deep breathing

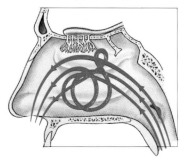

3. During deep breathing, although air swirls through the nose, little reaches the top of the nose spaces.

You sniff when you want to smell something particularly well, because a sniff will carry air and odor molecules higher up in your nose. The olfactory epithelium—the part of the lining of your nose that detects smells—is tucked away in two deep grooves (the olfactory clefts) at the very top of your nose. Above each patch of epithelium is an olfactory "bulb," a concentration of nerve cells that transmit nerve messages about smell directly to the brain.

When a sniff carries air up into the olfactory clefts, you get the maximum number of odor molecules hitting the ends of the sense cells in the epithelium. This means that the smell will be as strong as possible. When this happens, the sense cells send messages to the brain (via the olfactory bulb) that smells of a particular sort are arriving in the nose.

Ordinary breathing takes some odor to the olfactory clefts, so sometimes a new smell will take you by surprise. But most of the air bypasses these grooves during ordinary breathing and goes more directly toward the windpipe (trachea). Careful smelling needs careful sniffing.

100

Why does hay fever make people sneeze?

Hay fever is an over-energetic response from a person's body to something which is not an invading germ. When sensibly switched on, the defenses of the body attack and destroy disease-causing germs such as viruses and bacteria. What switches the system on is the arrival in the body of something it recognizes as "foreign." Such foreigners, or antigens, are usually substances like proteins on germ surfaces that are not a normal part of the body.

In hay fever, the defenses of the eyes and the lining of the nose are switched on not by germs but by tiny particles in the air you inhale. If you become sensitive to antigens in things like pollen grains from flowers, skin fragments from pet fur or bird feathers, or debris from mites that live in house dust, you may get "hay fever": it is not necessarily a reaction to cut grass or hay.

Your eyes itch and water, so does your nose and the irritation can make you sneeze. All this happens because the eyes and nose respond to the antigens by becoming inflamed and producing large amount of watery secretions.

A wide range of air-borne pollutants can provide the foreign bodies or antigens to which hay-fever sufferers become sensitive.

One of the commonest causes, the one which gives hay fever its name, is pollen. Pollen grains from grasses, trees and other plants reach high levels in the air we breathe in summer and early autumn.

Indoors, in the home, pollen levels are low, but other materials can cause a kind of hay fever. Antigens are found in hair, fur, feathers and, most surprisingly, in microscopic animals called mites that live in the ordinary house dust found in almost all homes.

Why is my nose lined with hairs?

Air breathed in through the nostrils has to pass through large spaces in the nose before it reaches the lungs. The moist folded walls of the airspaces mean that the inhaled air is moistened and pre-warmed before it gets to the lungs' delicate air sacs.

The wet coating of the airspaces and the moist hairs together trap air-borne dust particles so that the air is also cleaned and filtered. The dust in the watery mucus film of the airspaces gets passed eventually to the back of the throat where it is swallowed.

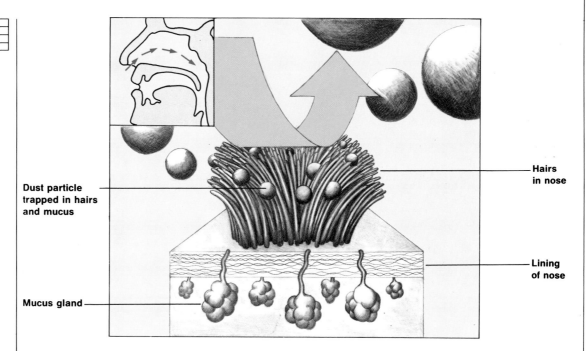

Dust particle trapped in hairs and mucus

Hairs in nose

Lining of nose

Mucus gland

The hairs in your nose are there to act as a filter for the air you breathe in. Besides being the sense organ of smell, the nose is the main route for air to get in and out of your lungs. The air sacs (alveoli) deep inside your lungs are delicate structures which are easily damaged. So the nose helps to clean up the air before it gets passed into the lungs. It also warms it.

The carpet of hairs inside the nose is kept moist by the secretions of numerous glands there which make the watery substance mucus. The wet hairs act like fly-papers to trap tiny dust particles which are wafted in with inhaled air. Only after this cleaning process does the air reach the windpipe and then get down into the lungs themselves.

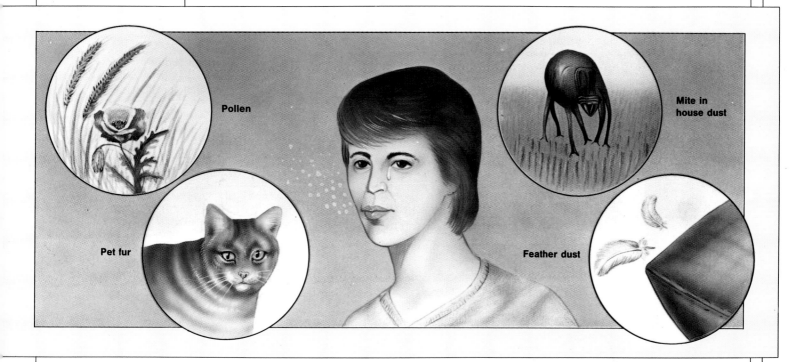

Pollen

Mite in house dust

Pet fur

Feather dust

102

What is my tongue for?

Your tongue is used for licking and tasting, chewing and swallowing, as well as for speaking. It is packed with muscles stretching in all directions which enable it to make the complicated movements needed for all these different uses.

Covering the tongue's upper surface is a bumpy soft skin, known as an epithelium. The individual bumps, called papillae, carry sense cells that enable you to taste flavors in your mouth.

In moving food around your mouth, your tongue puts the food where your teeth can chop and crush it; it then pushes the food to the back of your mouth when you're ready to swallow it.

Your tongue, working with your lips, also shapes sounds from your voicebox (in your throat) into words.

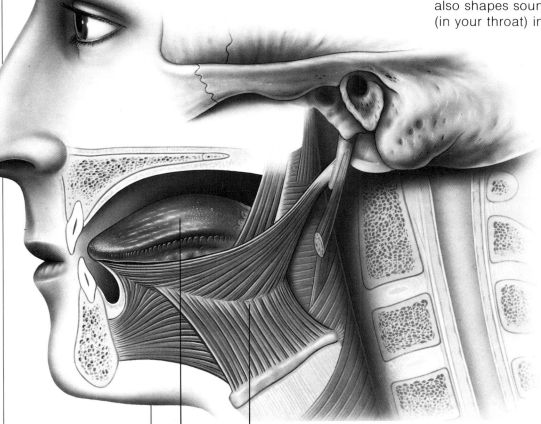

Tongue **Muscles for tongue movement**

The tongue is shown here in cutaway view from the left side, so that you can see the great complexity of muscles in and around the tongue. These muscles allow the tongue to change its shape and position with ease.

The tongue itself is made largely of criss-crossing muscle fibers. It is also joined by muscles to the bones of the lower jaw, the palate and to tiny bones near the Adam's apple (larynx).

103

Why does my food taste funny when I have a cold?

Most people are aware that their food has an odd taste, or no taste at all, when they have a cold or flu. But this is not because these illnesses actually alter the sense cells on your tongue.

The answer lies not in the tongue but in the runny nose you have with a cold. The lining of the nose makes far more watery mucus than usual, which is why you are forever blowing your nose. The mucus also stops you from smelling properly, and smell is a significant and important part of the "taste" of food.

When you say food tastes good you are really describing its flavor and smell together. If the smell part of this experience of senses disappears for a while, your food will taste boring.

You can test this for yourself. With your nose and eyes working, it is easy to "taste" the difference between pieces of apple, potato and onion in your mouth. Try the test blindfolded with a nose-clip on—you will find it far more difficult!

What is a taste bud?

A taste bud is a microscopic bundle of sense cells found on the surface of the tongue; they are sensitive to tastes. The little bumps you can see on the upper surface of your tongue are not taste buds, they are bulges of skin called papillae. The taste buds themselves are clustered in the skin around the base of these papillae. Each one is connected to a main nerve by a small bundle of nerve fibers.

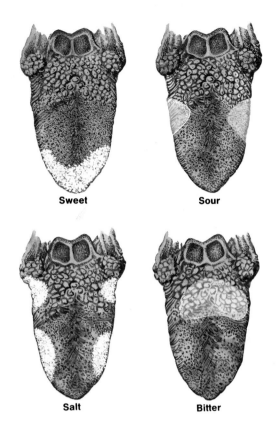

Sweet   **Sour**

Salt   **Bitter**

Microscopic taste buds sit in the lining of the upper surface of the tongue. They are made of layers of cells like the layers of an onion.

— **Sense cell of taste bud**

— **Taste bud entrance**

— **Sensory nerve fibers**

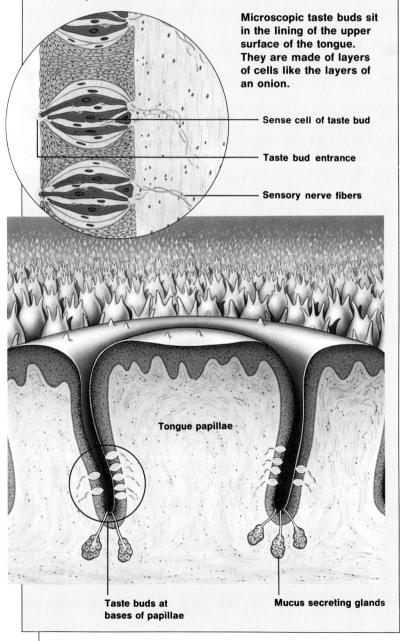

Tongue papillae

Taste buds at bases of papillae

Mucus secreting glands

How do I tell one taste from another?

The sense cells in the tongue's taste buds can respond to about four basic kinds of taste—sweet, sour, salty and bitter. The overall taste sensation you experience in your mouth is in fact a mixture of these tastes.

Each taste bud has a tiny pore in its top. Through this, the tips of the sense cells in each bud come into contact with taste substances in food, and are stimulated by them.

As the four diagrams above show, the taste buds in different parts of the tongue are especially sensitive to the main types of flavor. Many substances can have the same broad taste: sugar and saccharin, for instance, contain different chemical ingredients but both taste sweet. It is only when your taste buds work with your sense of smell that you can obtain a more precise taste.

What does my brain look like?

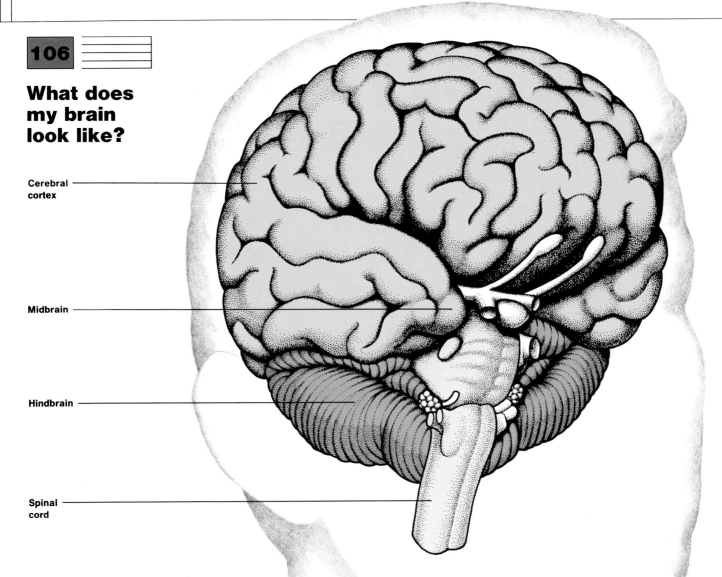

Cerebral cortex

Midbrain

Hindbrain

Spinal cord

It you could actually look inside your skull at the living brain, it would look rather like half a gigantic gray walnut kernel covered in a mesh of fine red blood vessels.

The walnut appearance is caused by the structure of the largest single section of the brain, called the cerebral cortex. This is the brain's control center, where messages are sorted and decisions taken about what to do. It sits on top of all the other parts, rather like a wig. Its surface is thrown into a series of deep grooves and ridges which make it look like the walnut. As on the nut, the pattern is symmetrical, with left and right halves of the cortex having mirror-image grooves.

Tucked under the rear edge of the "wig" of the cortex is the hindbrain,

including the cerebellum. It, too, is covered in grooves. Emerging from the hindbrain area is the spinal cord. The top of the spinal cord joins the rest of the nervous system to the brain, and just above this junction is the tiny midbrain. This is hidden from outer view and is made of several vital bundles of nerves that link together the different sections of the brain.

The pituitary gland, which controls the making of many of the body's hormones (chemical messengers), is near this region.

All the different parts of the brain are made up of nerve cells and the hollow center is filled with a liquid. The brain itself, inside the skull, is surrounded by a series of protective membranes, called the meninges.

107

Is the brain really a kind of computer?

A present-day computer and a brain have some things in common but there are also many differences.

Both are information-handling "machines" which operate by complicated networks of electrical activity—nerve impulses in the brain and tiny current-flows in microchips in a computer. Both have ways of taking in information (sense organs or a keyboard) and a memory for holding information. Both have "outputs" too—that is, they can make things happen as a result of their activity.

The differences between brains and computers have to do with their complexity and speed. Your brain is infinitely more complex than any computer in terms of the range of jobs it can carry out at the same time and in the way it can handle problems it has not tackled before. Its ability to learn cannot be matched by even the most sophisticated of today's computers.

Computers win out when they have to do large numbers of calculations extremely quickly and without mistakes. Scientists do not know yet if computers in the future may get so fast and complex that they will start to approach the abilities of the human brain.

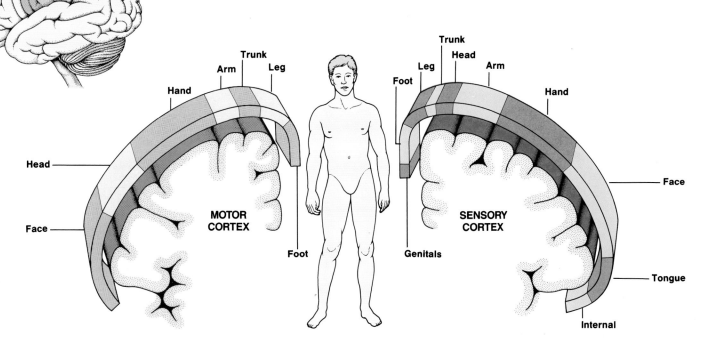

108

Do different parts of the brain do different jobs?

Yes they do. Certain types of job are carried out by particular parts of the brain, but others depend on different sections of the brain operating together.

The cerebral cortex, for instance, has zones concerned with the feelings we get from our sense organs. At the back of the cortex—strangely, as far from the eyes as possible—is the visual cortex, the section that enables us to see. At the sides of the cortex are similar sections for hearing.

Stretching across the top of the middle section of the cortex, like a pair of headphones, are two parallel stripes of brain tissue. The stripe called the motor cortex sends out the messages that control muscle movements in all parts of the body. The sensory-cortex stripe controls the body's sense of touch.

It is interesting to see the relative importance of different areas of the body in these control centers, as shown in the illustrations above. The tongue, for example, although physically a small area, needs to be given a larger part of the sensory cortex than, say, the trunk.

The cerebellum is our "auto-pilot" machinery which automatically co-ordinates our muscle movements and balance. Other brain sections, in or near the midbrain, control things such as wakefulness, emotions, hunger and pain.

Fish

Frog

Bird

Cat

109

Are all brains the same size?

All adult human brains are around the same size when you compare individuals of the same body size: the brains of women and men and those of people from different parts of the world.

All vertebrates, or animals with backbones—that is, fish, amphibians, reptiles, birds and mammals—have brains made of three basic parts: a hindbrain, a midbrain and a forebrain. The human brain is no exception. Its cerebral cortex is

an expansion of part of the forebrain.

The size of a brain depends on the size of the animal—bigger animals in general have bigger brains. But it also depends on the type of animal. Simpler vertebrates like fish have smaller brains in proportion to their size than birds or mammals do.

The proportions of the brain sections are also different in various types of animals. This is especially obvious in the amount and complexity of the cerebral

110

How do I remember things?

To remember something, you must first have learnt it, by picking up information from the outside world as sensations of sound, sight, smell, taste, touch.

The brain grasps a sensation just long enough for it to leave an impression. It keeps the information so that, for example, you still remember the beginning of a sentence by the time you reach the end. This is your "working memory" in operation, which is essential for short-term needs such as remembering a telephone number while you dial it.

Remembering things for longer than a minute or so requires effort. Your "long-term" memory holds onto how you do

things (such as riding a bicycle), events you have experienced (such as a visit to the zoo), and general knowledge (the capital city of Australia).

How you remember these things depends on how and where you learned them. Thus being in a certain room may bring "forgotten" memories flooding back; and seeing old friends in a photograph will immediately bring their names to mind.

Scientists are working to discover the mechanisms of memory. Certainly your memory relies upon chemicals and signals passing between nerve cells in your brain. However, the answer to this question is certainly not simple.

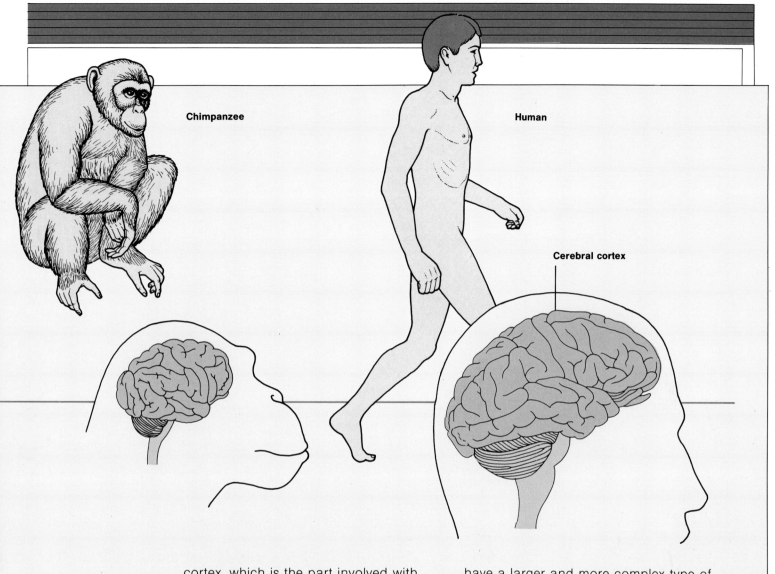

Chimpanzee

Human

Cerebral cortex

cortex, which is the part involved with intelligence and learned behavior. It hardly exists at all in fish and frogs and is small in birds, since these vertebrates behave mainly according to instinct.

Mammals such as cats and monkeys

have a larger and more complex type of cortex. But humans have the biggest and most complex of all, with many grooves and furrows and covering almost all other parts of the massive brain. This makes people the most intelligent of mammals.

111

How does my brain tell my body how to move?

It does so by a whole string of events that can happen in less than a second. A movement may begin from a conscious thought—for instance, if you decide to write a letter to your best friend, that is a conscious thought. The logical part of the cerebral cortex in your brain's "intelligence center" comes to the obvious conclusion that, to do this, you will need to pick up your pen—another conscious thought. At this point, thoughts have to be turned into actions and actions usually take the form of muscle movements.

As you decide to pick up your pen, your motor cortex, the part of your cerebral cortex involved with "doing," is sending

nerve messages to the muscles of the arm and fingers—scores of different muscles in all. They will all have to act in a controlled way, and in the right sequence, for you to pick up the pen.

Control of the accuracy of your movements is achieved by sight and by the position sense of your arm and hand, plus the sense of touch in your fingers. These vital pieces of sense information are handled by other sections of the cerebral cortex.

Coordinating the sense information and the commands to muscles is the job of the cerebellum, which works in partnership with the cerebral cortex.

112

Why are some people right-handed and others left-handed?

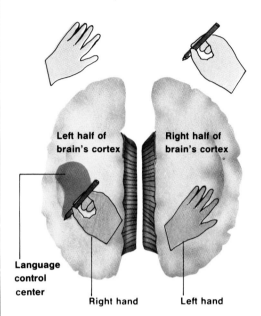

Left half of brain's cortex

Right half of brain's cortex

Language control center

Right hand

Left hand

The grooved surfaces of the two halves of the brain's cerebral cortex look like a walnut kernel. Each half controls the opposite side of the body. In right-handed people language control is located in the left side of the cortex, while in left-handed people it is found in the right side.

The hand that you choose to write with depends on which side of your brain is in charge of spoken and written language. For most people, it is the left half of the top of the brain (the cerebral cortex) that controls written and spoken words. And, strangely, the left half of the human brain drives the right half of the body and the right side of the brain drives the left! This is because, deep in the brain, the nerves from its two halves switch sides.

Most people then, have language control in the left cortex of their brain and are right-handed. Fewer people have the right half of their brain in charge of language and these people write with their left hand. Although left-handed people are in a minority, they are in no way handicapped because of this.

In right-handed people, number skills and logical reasoning are also handled in the left half of the brain while musical and artistic skills are mainly controlled by the right half. In left-handed people these jobs change sides also.

113

Does my brain close down when I go to sleep?

No! Unlike a computer with the plug pulled out, your brain does not switch itself off when you sleep. Instead it changes to a different way of working from the one it uses when you are awake.

While you sleep you are not responding to the outside world as you normally would. Thoughts are still happening in your head, though. We know this because of the way our nights are occupied with dreams. While you are asleep, you go through stages or cycles of deeper and shallower sleep. In the shallower periods

you are in dreaming sleep. This is also known as "rapid eye movement" or REM sleep because your eyes quickly flicker under the lids at this time. If you are woken during rapid eye movement sleep you will be in the middle of a dream.

Dreams are very mysterious things. Although we all probably have them every night, nobody really understands why. Some scientists think they happen because the brain tries to organize all the previous day's experiences into sensible patterns before starting the next day.

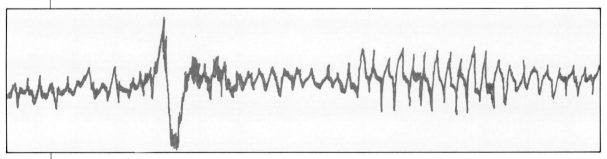

By attaching the heads of sleepers to electrodes (which connect the surface of the body electrically to a machine), you can tell when people are dreaming, although the electrodes do not pick up the dreams themselves! Instead they note the rapid eye movements that happen in dreaming sleep. The sharp zigzag trace, above, shows these movements.

Why do my eyes play tricks on me sometimes?

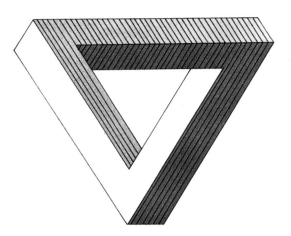

The impossible triangle fools the brain because the shading suggests a structure that cannot exist in three dimensions.

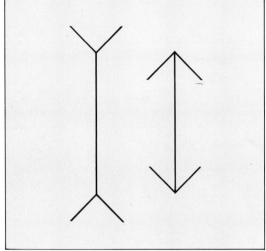

The two central lines are the same length although the angle lines give distance clues that make the left hand line look longer.

Seeing is not necessarily believing! The eye is not like a camera – it does not simply record light patterns. Seeing is a process carried out by your eyes and brain working together. Your eyes pick up light and use it to create signals which are sent to the brain. You can only see something when the brain has received and interpreted these signals.

The brain does this by remembering what visual patterns made sense in the past. It knows, for example, that objects closer to you will seem larger than those of the same size which are situated further away.

Some pictures can fool the brain's visual skills by giving false or confusing clues about an object's distance or its outer edges. This is what produces optical illusions, three examples of which are shown here.

Here you will find your mind flipping between two possibilities. Is this a bright goblet seen against a dark backdrop or two faces silhouetted against a light background?

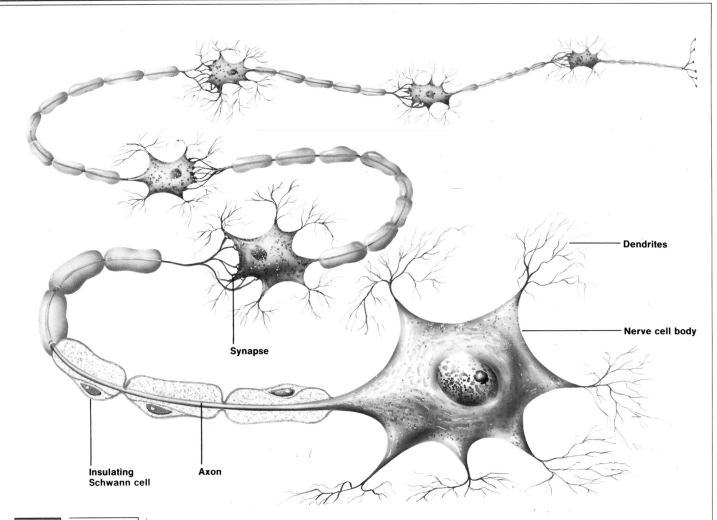

Dendrites

Nerve cell body

Synapse

Insulating
Schwann cell

Axon

What are nerves?

Nerves are the "wiring system" that controls all our activities and allows one part of the body to signal to another. Organized into thin, woven fibers that run from the brain to all parts of the body, the nerves even look like electrical wiring.

All nerves are made up of thousands of individual nerve cells called neurons, each of which can almost instantaneously transmit a "message" or nerve impulse along its length. Nerve impulses passing along nerves can run from one end of the body to the other in a minute fraction of a second.

Most nerves run to and from the brain, which is itself made up of nerve cells, organized into a large, interwoven mass. The brain is the "control center" of the whole nervous system—a type of living computer that receives messages from all over the body. It has a memory of past events and controls new activity by sending messages down other nerves.

Your nervous system contains billions of

The chain of nerve cells are linked together by nerve fibers. Covering the message-transmitting axons, like the plastic covering on a wire, is a row of sausage-shaped insulating cells known as Schwann cells.

nerve cells, but they are all built in more or less the same way. Each cell has a long "transmission cable" called an axon. It also has many other shorter projections called dendrites which make connections with other nerve cells.

The axon is surrounded by insulating cells that enable nerve impulses to pass quickly along it. Each nerve impulse is an electrical charge that moves quickly along the axon. It is triggered off when electrically charged atoms of sodium (sodium ions) rush into the cell.

A message is passed from one cell to another at places where they almost touch, called synapses. Each nerve impulse has to jump across the gap. It does this by causing a chemical trigger to start a new impulse in the next nerve cell.

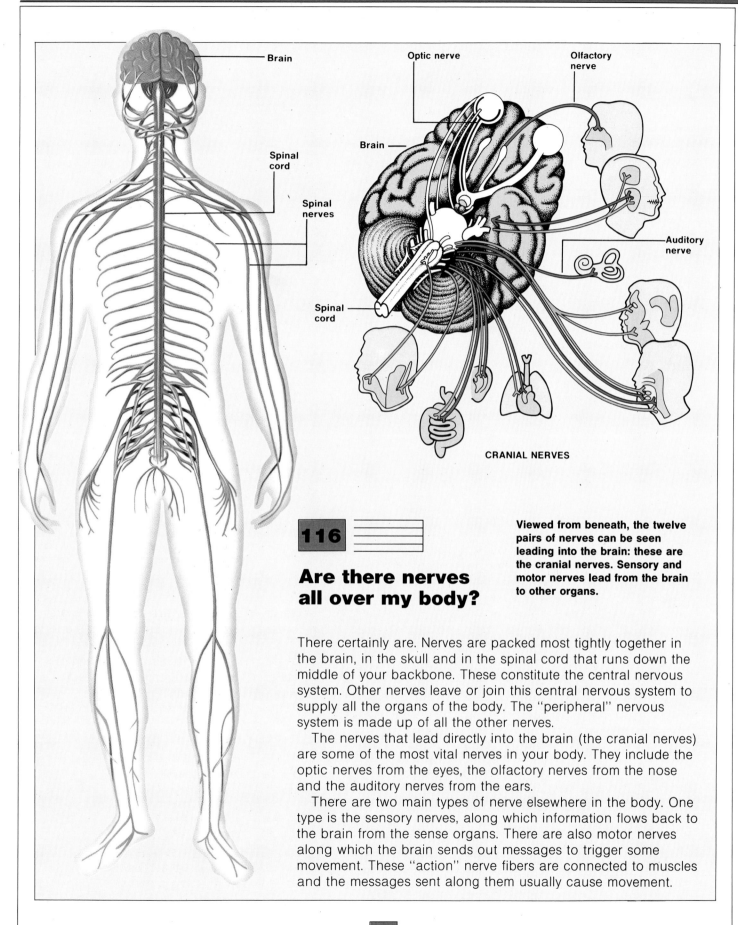

Brain

Optic nerve

Olfactory
nerve

Brain

Spinal
cord

Spinal
nerves

Auditory
nerve

Spinal
cord

CRANIAL NERVES

116

Are there nerves
all over my body?

**Viewed from beneath, the twelve
pairs of nerves can be seen
leading into the brain: these are
the cranial nerves. Sensory and
motor nerves lead from the brain
to other organs.**

There certainly are. Nerves are packed most tightly together in
the brain, in the skull and in the spinal cord that runs down the
middle of your backbone. These constitute the central nervous
system. Other nerves leave or join this central nervous system to
supply all the organs of the body. The "peripheral" nervous
system is made up of all the other nerves.

The nerves that lead directly into the brain (the cranial nerves)
are some of the most vital nerves in your body. They include the
optic nerves from the eyes, the olfactory nerves from the nose
and the auditory nerves from the ears.

There are two main types of nerve elsewhere in the body. One
type is the sensory nerves, along which information flows back to
the brain from the sense organs. There are also motor nerves
along which the brain sends out messages to trigger some
movement. These "action" nerve fibers are connected to muscles
and the messages sent along them usually cause movement.

117

Why do I jump if I step on a tack?

When you step on something sharp or painful a number of things appear to happen all at the same time. You feel a sharp pain in your foot. Also, without thinking about it, you quickly pull your foot away from the thing that has hurt you. You may also then draw your breath in sharply, or say "Ouch!", and look down to see what caused the pain. Only this last reaction in the sequence involves you in consciously thinking about what you are doing. The rest happens automatically.

The part of the body involved in all these reactions is your nervous system. First, when the tack presses into your skin, it stimulates sensitive nerve endings in your foot that signal damage. These nerve signals pass along sensory (receiving or sensing) nerves to the nearest part of the

spinal cord within your backbone. From here, further nerve messages pass out simultaneously in two different directions.

Some messages go up the spinal cord to the brain where they reach the part of the brain called the thalamus, which controls the feeling of pain. Once the nerve message reaches the thalamus you feel a sharp pain in the spot where the tack did its damage.

At the same time a second message goes out from the spinal cord. It travels along a motor (or doing) nerve to the muscles in your leg and "tells" them to lift your foot. This is a protective reflex which happens quite automatically, without you being aware that it is going to occur. The nerve signals that bring it about are called a reflex arc.

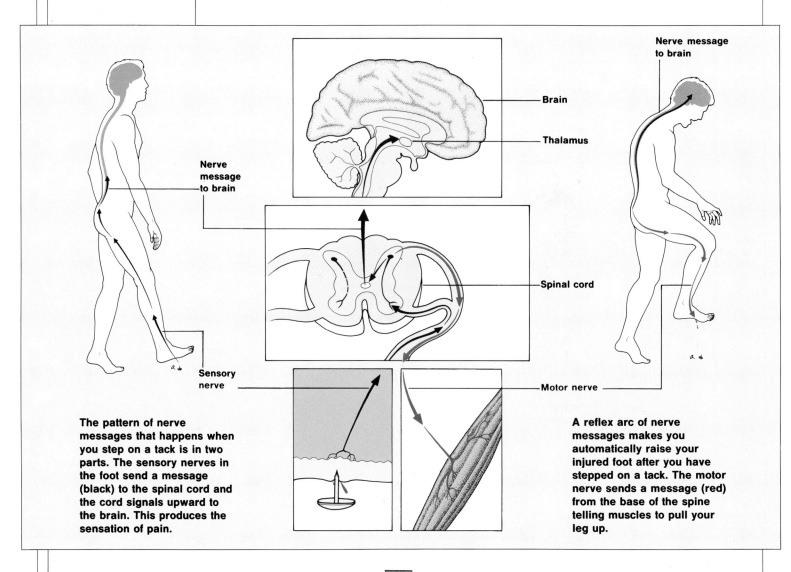

The pattern of nerve messages that happens when you step on a tack is in two parts. The sensory nerves in the foot send a message (black) to the spinal cord and the cord signals upward to the brain. This produces the sensation of pain.

A reflex arc of nerve messages makes you automatically raise your injured foot after you have stepped on a tack. The motor nerve sends a message (red) from the base of the spine telling muscles to pull your leg up.

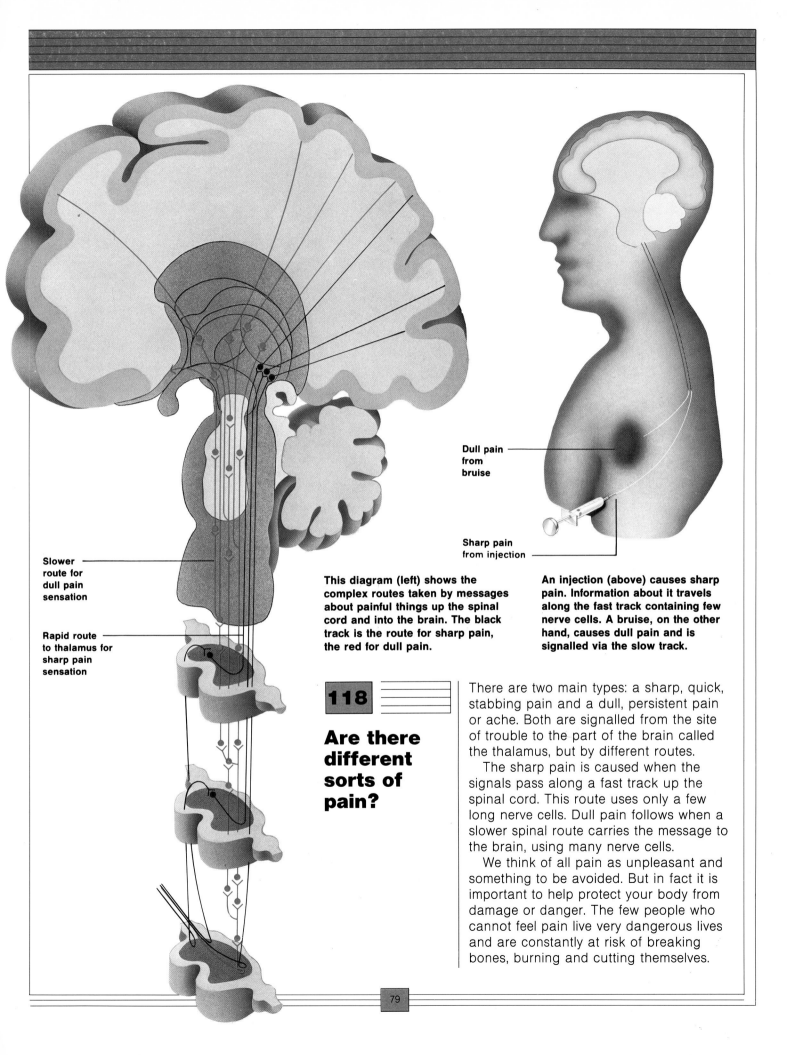

Slower route for dull pain sensation

Rapid route to thalamus for sharp pain sensation

This diagram (left) shows the complex routes taken by messages about painful things up the spinal cord and into the brain. The black track is the route for sharp pain, the red for dull pain.

Dull pain from bruise

Sharp pain from injection

An injection (above) causes sharp pain. Information about it travels along the fast track containing few nerve cells. A bruise, on the other hand, causes dull pain and is signalled via the slow track.

118

Are there different sorts of pain?

There are two main types: a sharp, quick, stabbing pain and a dull, persistent pain or ache. Both are signalled from the site of trouble to the part of the brain called the thalamus, but by different routes.

The sharp pain is caused when the signals pass along a fast track up the spinal cord. This route uses only a few long nerve cells. Dull pain follows when a slower spinal route carries the message to the brain, using many nerve cells.

We think of all pain as unpleasant and something to be avoided. But in fact it is important to help protect your body from damage or danger. The few people who cannot feel pain live very dangerous lives and are constantly at risk of breaking bones, burning and cutting themselves.

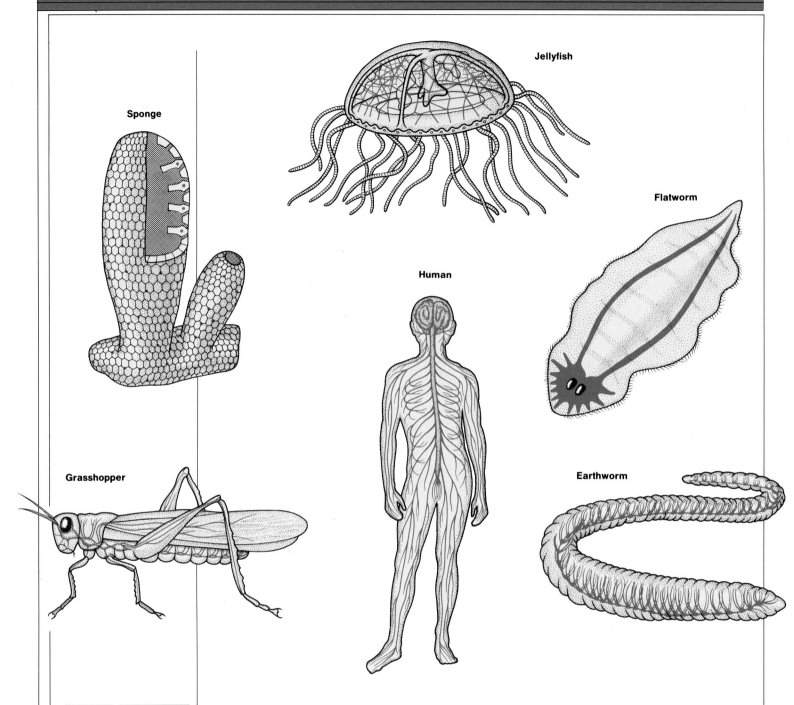

Sponge

Jellyfish

Flatworm

Human

Grasshopper

Earthworm

119

Do all creatures have nerves?

Almost all animals have nerves, though plants and microbes do not. The only animals that do not use a nervous system to control their actions and find out about the world around them are sponges and single-celled creatures such as ameba.

The nervous system in other animals may be simple or complicated. In a jellyfish, the nerves run around the body in a mesh called a nerve net – there is no brain. But most other animals have split their nervous system into a brain (a control center) and nerve fibers that carry messages to and from the brain. There are usually two kinds of nerve fibers. Sensory nerves provide the brain with information from the senses. Motor nerves let the brain make muscles move.

Flatworms, earthworms, and insects such as the grasshopper have brains and main nerve bundles that run from the front to the rear of their bodies. We ourselves have a large brain, a main nerve bundle (the spinal cord) running through the backbone, and other nerves that go to all parts of the body.

Anesthetics can be given in a number of ways. They can be breathed in, injected or sprayed on. General anesthetics are administered either as gases that are breathed in, or as injections. Local anesthetics are injected where they are needed: epidurals for a pain-free childbirth are given in the space around the spinal cord. Anesthetic sprays deaden small areas of skin for a while.

120

How does the doctor put me to sleep?

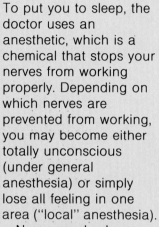

To put you to sleep, the doctor uses an anesthetic, which is a chemical that stops your nerves from working properly. Depending on which nerves are prevented from working, you may become either totally unconscious (under general anesthesia) or simply lose all feeling in one area ("local" anesthesia).

Nerves work when electrical charges called nerve impulses pass rapidly along them. Anesthetic drugs work by interfering with these impulses or by stopping one nerve from "speaking" to another.

In medicine, general anesthetics are used to put people into a very deep sleep. Long operations can then be carried out on them painlessly, and they wake up with no memory of what has happened.

Local anesthetics are used to make one part of the body numb. An injection in the gum allows the dentist to drill a tooth painlessly.

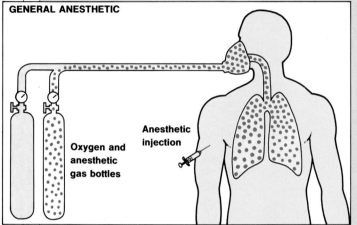

GENERAL ANESTHETIC

Oxygen and anesthetic gas bottles

Anesthetic injection

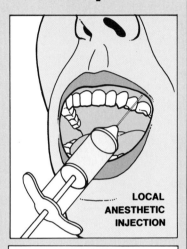

LOCAL ANESTHETIC INJECTION

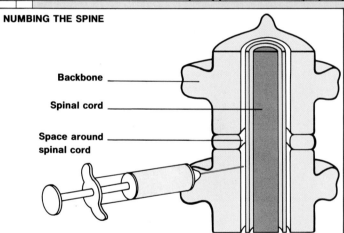

NUMBING THE SPINE

Backbone

Spinal cord

Space around spinal cord

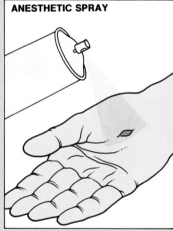

ANESTHETIC SPRAY

121

What happens when my hand or foot goes numb?

Everyone knows what it feels like when this happens. You have been sitting or lying in one position for some time. You then realize that you cannot feel your hand or foot. It has "gone to sleep." Not only can you not feel it, you will probably not be able to move it properly either. It feels as though it has been anesthetized.

What has happened is that the nerves to that part of your body have been squeezed by your weight so that they cannot pass nerve impulses properly. Squashed sensory nerves (the nerves that sense or feel things) mean that you cannot feel anything in that region. Squashed motor nerves (the nerves that work your muscles) mean that you cannot move there either.

Once you change position, the nerves quickly start operating again. With a few sharp tingles ("pins and needles") as the sensory nerves begin to transmit messages again, your hand or foot returns to normal. Slowly at first, you are soon able to move your fingers or your toes once again.

Why do I get shivers down my spine when I am frightened?

When you suddenly find yourself in a dangerous situation and are frightened, your nervous system's autopilot takes over and a whole series of changes happen in your body. In a situation of danger, your body cannot rely on you thinking about the right way to respond, so the correct response is produced instinctively and immediately by your body's autonomic or autopilot system.

When your brain is alerted by fear, the glands above the kidneys, called the adrenal glands, release a powerful hormone called adrenaline (epinephrine) into the bloodstream. This causes changes which make your body ready to defend itself or to run away from the danger—for "fight or flight."

First of all, the adrenaline causes your muscles to tense up. This can make them ache or even tremble, which is why people are said to quiver with fear. At the same time the blood vessels get narrower in

some places and wider in others. The vessels taking blood to your muscles relax so that more fuel-carrying blood can get to them. The others get narrower in compensation, which makes your face and other areas of your skin go white—they are temporarily starved of blood.

Your heart beats faster so that enough extra blood can be pumped to the muscles. And you breathe faster. This gets more oxygen into your body which is needed for all the extra work it will have to do in "fight or flight."

The nerve and hormone changes of fright make several other things happen. Your mouth goes dry and you sweat, even though your body is feeling cold, not hot. The palms of your hands go especially clammy since they are well supplied with sweat glands. At the same time your hairs stand on end and you get the shivery feeling, or shivers down the spine, associated with fear.

How fast are my reactions?

Your "reaction time" is how long it takes you to start doing something once you have been given the signal to begin. The actual time depends on the type of signal and the kind of action required, as well as your training for this. For most simple activities, your reaction time is about 150–200 milliseconds, that is between fifteen hundredths and one fifth of a second (a millisecond is a thousandth of a second).

The reaction time of an Olympic sprinter at the start of a 100-meter race is an exciting example of fast reaction times. Think what has to happen in the reaction

time. The runner's ears pick up the sound of a gun, nerves from the ear pass a message to the brain and the brain sends nerve messages to the leg muscles to start running. A good sprinter's reaction time from hearing the gun to starting to move is around 200 milliseconds.

Reaction times in a race are automatically recorded by the electronic starting blocks. If the time is less than 110 milliseconds, it is termed a false start: the runner must have decided to go before hearing the gun. Some sprinters are now getting close to this timing.

Why do I get hiccups?

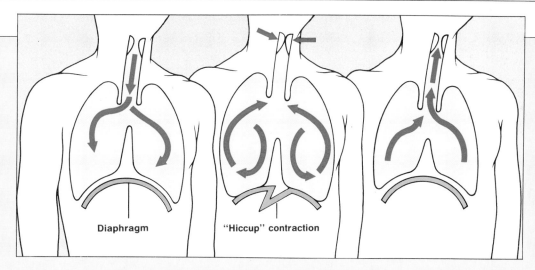

Diaphragm   "Hiccup" contraction

During each hiccup the domed muscle of the diaphragm contracts and twitches. This sudden contraction sucks air quickly into the lungs. The resulting noise is termed a hiccup.

Hiccups are sudden noisy intakes of air that happen when the muscles of the diaphragm twitch. The cause is not always known, but it could be triggered off by an irritation in the stomach, or by eating or drinking too much, or too quickly.

The diaphragm is a curved sheet of muscle at the base of your ribcage and underneath your lungs. The work done by this muscle expands the lungs and helps you breathe in. If the diaphragm starts twitching, each twitch produces a sharp intake of breath. A flap of tissue in your throat, which is part of your voicebox, then snaps shut, cutting off the air flow and making the typical hiccup sound. The flap, called the epiglottis, then opens, and you breathe out.

Hiccups usually stop of their own accord, but there are many folk remedies for them. One is holding your breath, and another is drinking a glass of water with your hands held over your ears (you need help with this!).

At the 1987 World Championships in Rome, Ben Johnson (right) had a staggeringly fast reaction time of 129 milliseconds. That start helped him to gain a new World Record for the race, of 9.83 seconds.

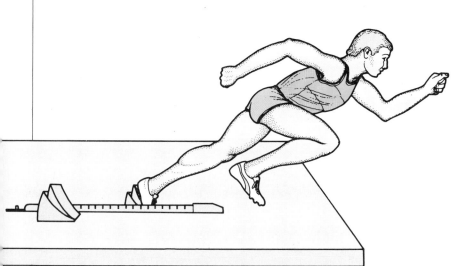

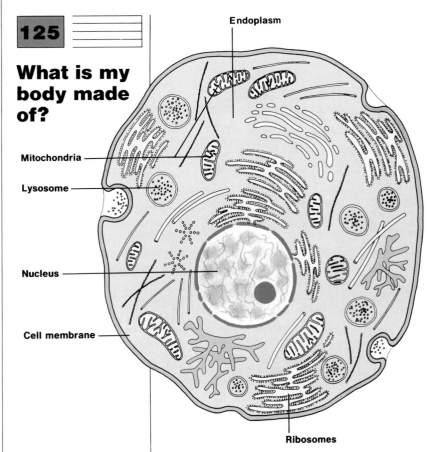

125

What is my body made of?

Endoplasm

Mitochondria

Lysosome

Nucleus

Cell membrane

Ribosomes

Your body is made of microscopic building blocks called cells. There are billions of them, and more than one hundred different sorts. Each type groups together to make different body tissues.

A cell is a tiny unit of life, the smallest "building block," from which all living things are made. The simplest organisms consist of a single cell each, and larger animals and plants are composed of collections of cells. A cell can grow and it can split to make more cells like itself.

Each cell is surrounded by a cell membrane which is microscopically thin. In the center of the cell, wrapped in a double-thickness membrane coat, is the nucleus. This is the part of the cell that houses the genes. The genes contain the "plans," both for making new cells and to enable a cell to construct its own building materials—particularly new proteins.

The area of the cell surrounding the nucleus is called the cytoplasm. It contains its own mini-organs, known as "organelles." These include mitochondria, that provide energy, and ribosomes that can make new proteins.

126

How can the body fight off germs?

When germs such as bacteria are present in the body, "killer" white blood cells can leave blood vessels and eat bacteria in the surrounding tissues.

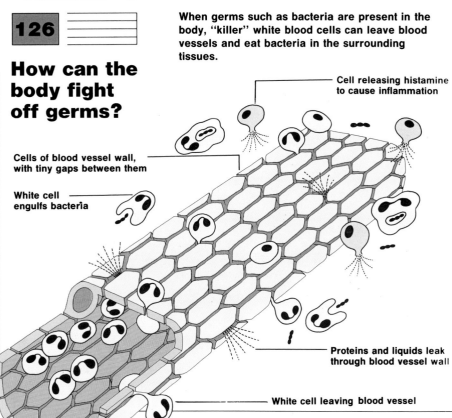

Cell releasing histamine to cause inflammation

Cells of blood vessel wall, with tiny gaps between them

White cell engulfs bacteria

Proteins and liquids leak through blood vessel wall

White cell leaving blood vessel

Your body fights off germs with its defensive machinery, called the immune system. The immune system has two main types of weapons which it can use against invading germs. The first are protective proteins called antibodies. The other is a collection of "killer cells" which can attach to germs and destroy them.

The immune system has two jobs: to recognize that germs have entered the body and to fight them off. The antibodies help in both these tasks. Germs are recognized as "foreign" because they have non-human proteins. Antibodies attach to them and brand the invader as a suitable enemy for the other parts of the immune system. It is as though the antibodies had painted a target on each germ for the killer cells to aim at.

Antibodies are made by a type of white blood cell called a B-cell lymphocyte. Other types of white blood cell act as "killer cells" or phagocytes. They eat the targeted germs by swallowing them into their cytoplasm and digesting them.

The diagram, right, illustrates just eleven of the hundreds of different specialist types of cell which are present in the human body.

The egg is one of the largest human cells, and the one from which, once fertilized, all the other cells come.

Epithelial or skinlike cells cover many spaces inside as well as outside the body. Here the epithelial cells lining the lung's airspaces and the tube-lining cells of the kidney's minute filters are shown.

There are many different kinds of gland cell in the body. The pancreas cells produce either digestive enzymes which are used in the gut or the hormone called insulin which is passed into the bloodstream to help the body make energy from sugars.

Blood is a fluid tissue which contains red and white cells, which float in the blood fluid or plasma.

Nerve cells and muscle cells are both very long. Nerve cells pass nerve messages around the body. Muscle cells are organized into muscles which move body parts.

Bone cells help to build the skeleton. They secrete the fibers and minerals from which bone is made.

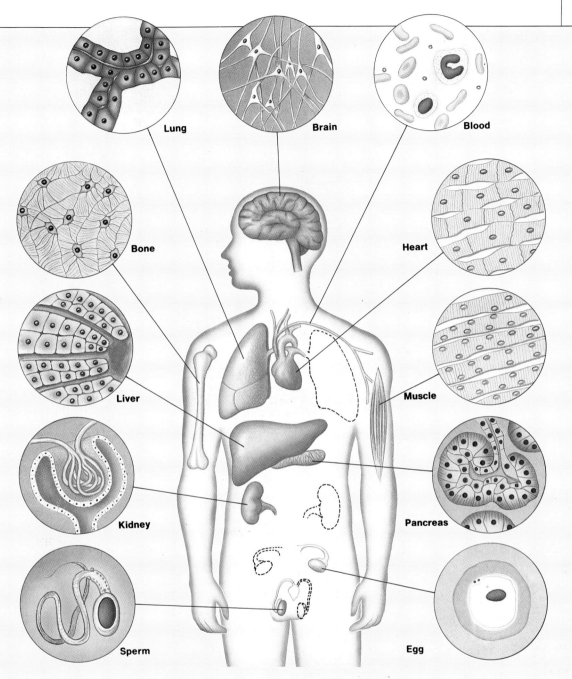

Lung

Brain

Blood

Bone

Heart

Liver

Muscle

Kidney

Pancreas

Sperm

Egg

127

How many different sorts of cells are there in my body?

There are hundreds of different sorts of cells in the body. But the main types are sex cells (eggs and sperm); muscle cells; nerve cells; epithelial (inner and outer skin) cells; blood cells; bone cells, cartilage and connective cells; and gland cells, specialized to produce a wide range of secretions.

You started life as a single cell, formed by an egg cell from your mother and a single sperm cell from your father. That one single cell, the fertilized egg, divided over and over again to produce the billions of cells from which you are made today. Some of the cells are still dividing, making new skin, blood, and hair for instance.

That one fertilized egg eventually gives rise to all the other cell types in your body, although all your cells have the same genes. This production of different cells is called differentiation. It happens because in various sorts of cells, different parts of the total "gene plan"—known to scientists as DNA—are switched on or off.

128

How does a vaccination work?

Vaccinations work by fooling the body's immune system. A vaccination is an injection which makes a person immune, or resistant, to a particular disease. After the vaccination, it is very difficult for the germs (viruses or bacteria) of that disease to infect the vaccinated person.

The injection makes the body think it is really being infected with a disease when, in fact, it is not. Tricked in this way, the body's immune system causes B-cell lymphocytes (a sort of white blood cell) to make protective antibodies. These antibodies can attach themselves to the real germs of the disease, should they ever be present. Killer cells are present in large numbers too, ready to attack them.

How does the vaccine manage this trick? The material being injected is made of substances very like those of the germs. If it is similar enough, the antibodies and cells of the body's defenses react as though fighting a proper infection.

The easiest way to make vaccines like this is to use dead or weakened germs which are harmless to people. But since these germs have almost the same chemical structure as live, dangerous ones, the immune system cannot work out the difference. It is also possible to make parts of germs by genetic engineering and these parts can be used as vaccines.

Good vaccines now exist for most of the so-called childhood diseases. With a correct vaccination program between birth and the age of about 11, it should be possible to protect all children against most of these diseases.

This graph shows average heights against age for growing boys and girls. It reveals several interesting things. Up until the age of about 11 there is little difference in the growth curves of girls and boys. Girls have an adolescent growth spurt in their early teens, just before boys do, but then their height levels off earlier. In the end, boys are, on average, taller than girls.

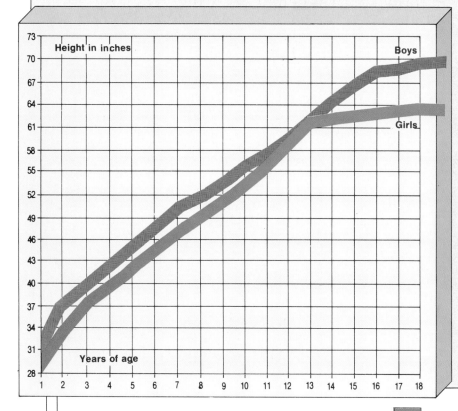

129

Can you tell how tall children will be when they grow up?

A simple way of judging roughly how tall you will be when you grow up is to look at your parents. Height is one of those things which, like the color of your eyes, hair and skin, you inherit from your mother and father. This will only give you an approximate idea of your final height, however. Your mother may be relatively short and your father tall, for example, in which case you may be like either—or somewhere in between.

Diet can also affect growth. Children who are undernourished through childhood will not grow to the full height their inherited genes would allow if they were adequately fed.

A more reliable way of estimating your grown-up height is to check your present height relative to your age against those on an age/height graph for average children. If you see how you compare to the average, it is likely that your general growth pattern will continue and this will enable you to make a good guess about your final height. Another approximate guide is that two-year-olds are roughly half their final grown-up height.

130

What are hormones?

Hormones are chemical messengers produced by your glands. Their messages are either sent short distances to a particular organ, or spread around the body in the bloodstream to influence many organs.

Hormones are one of the two main ways in which your body organizes and controls its activities. The other method is by nerve messages carried along nerves. These electrical messages move around extremely quickly and let your body have direct and immediate control over its actions.

Hormones control your body in a different way. These chemical messengers usually act more slowly and often produce changes in many parts of the body at once. They control subtle, complex, and more wide-ranging things like growth, sexual development and your body's metabolism.

Most hormones are either proteins or another type of organic molecule called a steroid. Insulin, one of the hormones that controls sugar levels in your body, is an example of a protein hormone. The sex hormones, which control sexual development, are steroids.

One of the most crucial hormone-making glands is the pituitary at the base of the brain. It has been called the "conductor of the hormone orchestra," since many of the hormones it produces control the actions of other hormone-secreting glands.

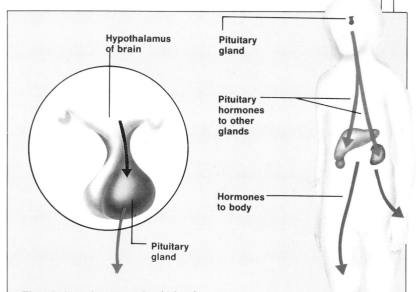

The pituitary is a pea-sized gland hanging from the base of the brain by a stalk. It has many nerve links with a region of the brain called the hypothalamus. This enables the pituitary to be partially controlled by the brain, so it is a link between nerve and hormone control of the body.

131

Why do our bodies stop growing?

Our bodies stop growing when the pituitary gland stops producing a special growth hormone. Your body knows when to stop growing because both the switching on and the switching off of growth is carefully organized by your brain working closely together with your pituitary gland.

All growth is controlled by hormones and the hormones that do the controlling are themselves controlled by other hormones. The total story is a very complicated one!

During the years of growth from birth until your late teens, a magic material, a hormone called GRF (the initials stand for growth hormone releasing factor) is made in the part of the brain known as the hypothalamus. GRF passes from the brain to the pituitary gland. Triggered by GRF, the gland makes growth hormone (somatotropin) which is carried around all of your body in the blood. In the liver and kidneys it is changed into a new form, called somatomedin, that can make you grow. It can, for instance, make bones lengthen.

At the end of adolescence—the period when a lot of physical and emotional changes have been taking place—a new "switch off" hormone called GIF (growth hormone inhibitory factor) is made in the brain. This stops the pituitary making growth hormone—so you stop growing.

132

When do I stop being a child?

Growing up, becoming an adult, is not something that takes place overnight but is something that happens gradually, over a period of time. This period is partly to do with physical changes in your body and partly to do with the ways you think and feel about yourself, other people, and the world around you. These changes mostly happen during your teenage years and are most obvious around the early teens—say from the ages of 11 to 15—during the period called adolescence or puberty.

The body changes in adolescence turn girls into young women who can have babies and boys into young men who can make women pregnant. The changes happen because of rising levels of sex hormones in your body.

In girls, breasts begin to grow, the body gets more shapely, periods start and hair grows under the arms and around the vaginal area. In boys, the voice gets deeper, the penis and testicles grow larger, and hair starts growing on the lower part of the face, under the arms and around the genitals.

133

Why do men have more hair on their bodies than women?

Probably so that it is easy to tell men and women apart! In many mammals—and people are mammals too—the male and female of a species look obviously different. Male elephant seals are vastly bigger than their mates; male deer have antlers while the hinds do not; male lions have a mane and lionesses do not. A similar situation is true for us—it is easy to distinguish women from men.

Men and women are different in size and shape: men are, on average, slightly broader than women and a little taller; women have a more rounded, curvy shape and have breasts. Besides these differences, though, perhaps the most obvious one is facial hair. If they did not shave, almost all men in the world would have a face in which only the eyes, mouth and nose were visible. Beard and moustache would cover the rest. Women, on the other hand, do not have hairy faces; they also have far less hair on their arms, legs and chest than men do.

We are not really sure why these differences have arisen in our evolution. The growth of facial hair and lots of body hair is the result of the rising male sex hormone levels in adolescence. Early in human evolution it was possibly useful for women to be able to see at a glance the difference between a sexually mature male and an immature one. The very hairy ones would have been the most mature males.

In the same way, the beard and body hair might have been a sort of "badge of maturity," used to signal who was most powerful in fights between males.

Some of the everyday functions of hormones are shown on the left of the illustration. They make sure, for example, that salt and sugar levels in the blood stay as they should, that our temperature is normal and that an egg is released from a woman's ovaries every month.

The changes shown on the right of the illustration happen automatically, as a result of hormone activity in response to danger.

The signalling comes from the pituitary gland, just beneath the brain, which releases a hormone called ACTH into the blood. When the hormone reaches the adrenal glands on top of the kidneys it kicks them into producing adrenaline (epinephrine) and other hormones that get the body ready for action.

Your heart speeds up, your lungs expand, the liver releases sugars for energy into the blood and the blood is switched to the muscles and away from other, non-vital places such as the digestive system to provide the maximum blood for action.

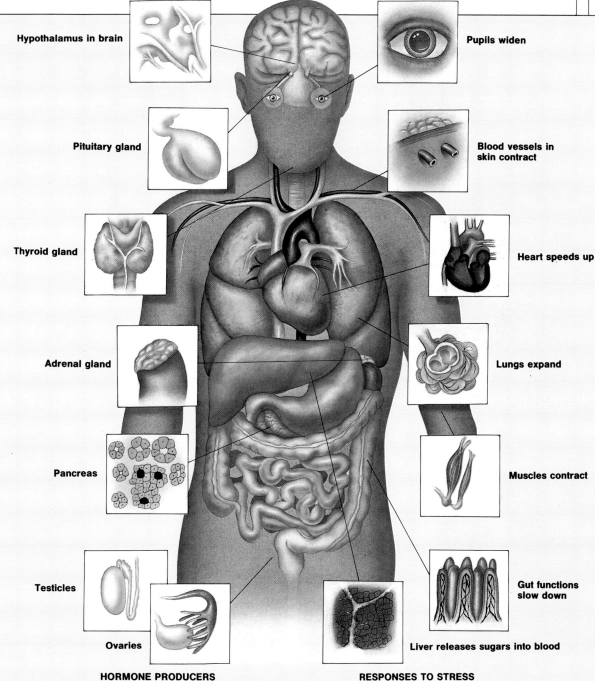

Hypothalamus in brain

Pupils widen

Pituitary gland

Blood vessels in skin contract

Thyroid gland

Heart speeds up

Adrenal gland

Lungs expand

Pancreas

Muscles contract

Testicles

Gut functions slow down

Ovaries

Liver releases sugars into blood

HORMONE PRODUCERS

RESPONSES TO STRESS

134

Does one part of my body control my reactions?

No, your reactions are the result of careful coordination by various parts of your body. But it is the job of nerves and hormones to relay messages from one part to another.

Some of the jobs that hormones do in your body are a sort of "housekeeping." They make sure that the normal, everyday body functions carry on steadily. Hormones are also crucial when we suddenly have to handle something new, stressful or dangerous. The sense messages about danger from our sense organs are sent to the control center or cortex of the brain. Nerve signals from the cortex can then cause two types of reaction.

Firstly, you may take specific action—you might run away from the trouble—and nerve messages from the brain's cortex will control the muscles that let you run. Secondly, your cortex signals to your hormone machinery to put you on "red alert"—ready for anything.

°F
98.7
98.5
98.3
98.1
97.9
97.7
97.5
Time
06.00   08.00   10.00   12.00   14.00   16.00

A bodily cycle which is easily measured is that of our temperature. Although we say a normal body temperature is 98.2° F (36.7° C), in reality it bounces up and down slightly. The total range is only about one degree Fahrenheit, but it is highest in the early evening and lowest in the early hours. Fluctuations in body temperature seem to be closely related to mental performance.

135

Why do we go to sleep at night and stay awake in the daytime?

We seem to have a "biological clock" in our bodies that enables us to tell the time of day. In other words, we have a built-in sleeping and waking rhythm which does not need outside clues like watches or the sun to make it work.

This cycle is, of course, reinforced in everyday life, where everyone around us is doing more or less the same thing at the same time. In a family routine, parents and children usually wake up at about the same time in the morning, because alarm clocks, parents' shouts and a general increase in noise will waken everyone.

But this is only a small part of the explanation. Scientific experiments have

136

Can drugs really make you run faster?

Yes, but it is both illegal and dangerous to use drugs in this way in sports. It is illegal because using drugs that help you perform well makes the competition unfair. It is dangerous because many of the drugs have serious side-effects. Athletes and sportsmen and women may take these drugs not realizing that eventually they may make them very ill. At present, in many types of international sports, big efforts are being made to catch sports drug-takers by doing tests on them.

Several kinds of drugs have been used in this way. Some stop you feeling tired and these have been used in endurance sports, such as running a marathon, where much stamina is needed. There are also stimulant drugs that make you feel very alert.

Another type are body-building drugs, used in sports where having a big, muscular body puts you at an advantage.

American football, weight-lifting and most throwing field events—like javelin, shot-put, discus and hammer—are all examples. The drugs currently in the news in this context are anabolic steroids, which act like growth hormones and make you increase your muscle bulk. Using these can certainly have dangerous side-effects.

One strange sort of "drug taking" in sport is the blood transfusion of the athlete's own blood. In long distance running, the ability of an athlete's blood to carry oxygen from lungs to muscles is very important. To boost this, some runners have had some of their blood removed and stored for months before an important race. Just before the race they have their own blood transfused back into their body. This gives them far more oxygen-carrying red blood cells than normal and their stamina increases significantly.

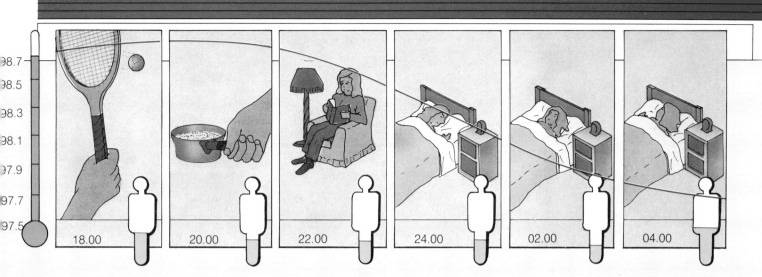

18.00	20.00	22.00	24.00	02.00	04.00

been done to show that, even when kept away from all possible clues—say, in a cave deep underground—people still stick to a roughly 24-hour sleeping and waking cycle. After sleeping for about eight hours, they will wake up—at around the same time every day.

Scientists have shown that there are other things, apart from sleeping, which happen automatically, and with a daily rhythm, in our bodies. Our body temperature goes up and down slightly according to the time of day; our production of urine happens mainly by day and falls to low levels at night; there is a 24-hour cycle in our work concentration,

shown for example in the varying speed and accuracy with which we can do mental arithmetic or other mental tasks at different times of day.

This built-in rhythm causes us problems when we travel rapidly around the world in fast jets. We get the effects of "jet-lag." If we travel east or west, our day becomes dramatically shorter or longer than the 24 hours for which we are programmed. When we arrive at our destination, with our body's clock still set for home time, we have to "reset" it, and it can take several days to become fully adjusted. This confuses the body and makes us feel unwell.

There is a rhythm to the changing levels of certain chemicals in our bloodstream. The tiny figure in the above illustrations indicates the fluctuating level of the hormone called cortisol through a 24-hour day. Cortisol helps to control many body activities, like the number of white cells in the blood, and the activities of heart and lungs.

137
Why do some children have to give themselves insulin injections?

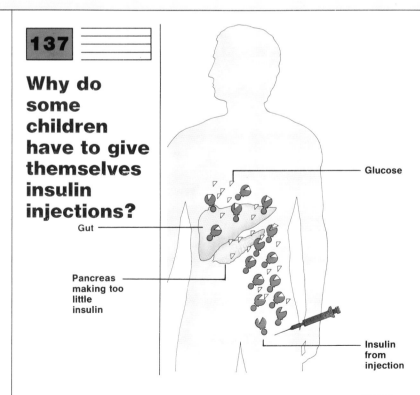

Glucose

Gut

Pancreas making too little insulin

Insulin from injection

It is because they are diabetics. Diabetes is a disease caused when the pancreas gland under the stomach stops producing enough of the hormone insulin. Insulin is one of the hormones that helps to control sugar levels in the blood. If there is not enough insulin, a diabetic can feel very ill or even go into a coma because their blood does not contain enough sugar.

The disease is one of the commonest of those that concern a hormone. About one in every hundred people is a diabetic. Luckily, since the 1920s, when the link between insulin and diabetes was discovered, it has been possible to treat the disease. Children who are diabetics are able to make up for their missing insulin by injecting themselves with insulin once or twice every day. This insulin top-up allows them to remain healthy.

Pure human insulin for the injections can now be made by genetic engineering.

Index

Page numbers in **bold** type indicate illustrations

Acknowledgments

Artwork by

Jill Elsbury   Frank Kennard
and

Norman Barber   John Bavosi   Louis Bory Associates
Michael Courtney   John Davies   Ken Goldammer
Mick Gillah   Tony Graham   Greensmith Associates
Dennis Hawkins   Ivan Hissey   Joyce Hurwitz   Aziz Kahn
Mel Petersen   Mark Seidler   Rob Shone   Les Smith
Norman Swift

Photographs by

26 Alfred Owczarzak/Taurus Photos
32 Chris Bigg
43 James Stevenson/Science Photo Library
83 Colorsport
88 John Bulmer